UK Drugs Unlimited

UK Drugs Unlimited

New Research and Policy Lessons on Illicit Drug Use

Edited by

Howard Parker
Professor and Director of SPARC
University of Manchester

Judith Aldridge
Lecturer in Criminology and Social Policy
University of Manchester

and

Roy Egginton
Research Associate
SPARC
University of Manchester

First published 2001 by
PALGRAVE
Houndmills, Basingstoke, Hampshire RG21 6XS and
175 Fifth Avenue, New York, N. Y. 10010
Companies and representatives throughout the world

PALGRAVE is the new global academic imprint of
St. Martin's Press LLC Scholarly and Reference Division and
Palgrave Publishers Ltd (formerly Macmillan Press Ltd).

ISBN 0–333–91817–7

This book is printed on paper suitable for recycling and
made from fully managed and sustained forest sources.

A catalogue record for this book is available
from the British Library.

Library of Congress Cataloging-in-Publication Data
UK drugs unlimited : new research and policy lessons on
illicit drug use / edited by Howard Parker, Judith Aldridge,
and Roy Egginton.
     p. cm.
Includes bibliographical references and index.
ISBN 0–333–91817–7
  1. Drug abuse—Great Britain. 2. Youth—Drug use—Great
Britain. I. Parker, Howard J. II. Aldridge, Judith, 1963–
III. Egginton, Roy.
HV5840.G7 I555 2000
362.29'0941—dc21
                                      00–066924

10   9   8   7   6   5   4   3   2   1
10 09 08 07 06 05 04 03 02 01

Printed in Great Britain by Antony Rowe Ltd, Chippenham, Wiltshire

Contents

List of Tables

List of Figures

Acknowledgements

Since the early 1990s SPARC has been helped by several thousand young people who have cooperated with our school surveys, nightclub study and interview investigations. We would like to thank them all. We would also like to thank our researcher interviewers' network especially: Lucy Attenborough, Jon Breeze, Tony Bullock, Catherine Bury, Tyrone Cole, Paul Doyle, Wendy Evans, Dean Herd, Tina James, Danny Knight, Mark Liggett, Ian McDonald, Laurence Milburn, Debbie Oates, Jaki Pugh, Craig Ruckledge, Sally Shenton, Maxine Smith and Chendi Ukwuoma.

We would like to thank the Home Office for allowing us to use data generated from research commissioned by them and the ESRC for two substantial grants and similarly Drugscope and the Department of Health.

Finally, we would like to express our gratitude to Dianne Moss who has been administrative secretary with SPARC throughout.

Notes on the Contributors

Judith Aldridge is Lecturer in Criminology and Social Policy at the University of Manchester. Her research centres around adolescent alcohol and recreational drug use, with particular interest in methodological and measurement issues. She is co-author of *Illegal Leisure: the normalisation of adolescent recreational drug use* (1998) and *Dancing on Drugs: Health Risk and Hedonism in the British Clubscene* (2000).

Tim Bottomley is a drugs service manager with Trafford Community Drugs Team. He was seconded to SPARC on two occasions to undertake the crack cocaine study (Chapter 7).

Kevin Brain is a Social Exclusion Policy officer with Warrington Unitary Authority. He is an Honorary Research Fellow with SPARC and was a research assistant during 1997–98.

Jon Breeze was a postgraduate student and part-time research assistant with SPARC (1997–99). He is currently a research associate at Sheffield Hallam University.

Roy Egginton is a social researcher with SPARC at the University of Manchester specialising in patterns of alcohol and drug use among young people. His most recent publications include: *'New heroin outbreaks amongst young people in England and Wales'* with H. Parker and C. Bury (1998) and *'Hidden Heroin Users: Young People's Unchallenged Journeys to Problematic Drug Use'* (with H. Parker, 2000).

Nicola Elson has worked as a research assistant for SPARC (1998–2000).

Howard Parker has a long and distinguished career as a social researcher. His first book *View From The Boys* (1974) has become a classic ethnographic study. Author of seven books, most recently he has, with SPARC colleagues, written *Illegal Leisure: the normalisation of adolescent* *recreational drug use* (1998) and *Dancing on Drugs: Health Risk and Hedonism in the British Clubscene* (2000).

Fiona Measham is now a lecturer in criminology at Lancaster University. She was a research fellow, then senior fellow, with SPARC, 1991–99.

Glossary

baghead	heroin user
the beat	neighbourhood or streets prostitutes frequent
brown(s)	heroin
clucking	withdrawing, once called turkeying
digging	injecting
earning	or grafting, making money illegally
gaff	own home, place to live. 'Your own gaff.'
gear	heroin
gouching	state of intoxication following administration of heroin
grafting	can mean just working hard but in drugs world refers to committing crime usually on a regular basis
honeymooning	initial period enjoying heroin (see gouching)
lines	lines of heroin on a foil to be heated or smoked
meth	methadone linctus
pinhead	injector but also a reference to eye pupil size
radgy	bad person, criminal 'scally'
rattling	withdrawing, once called turkeying
roasting	withdrawing from an addictive drug, usually heroin, without help
rocks	crack cocaine
sack	or 'sack off' meaning to give up or reject
smack	heroin
stone	another name for crack cocaine
white	cocaine in general, crack in particular in this study
works	heroin injecting equipment

Introduction

SPARC, a small multi-disciplinary drugs research centre at Manchester University, England, has been undertaking major studies into the UK drugs situation for a decade. In this book we attempt, for the first time, to draw together our collective efforts to describe and analyse the drugs situation in the UK. We begin in Chapter 1 by outlining how the United Kingdom has become the most drug-involved population in Europe and is now on a par with the USA. However, there are many different drugs arenas and populations, from adolescent drug triers to weekend dance drug users to general population, recreational drug users especially of cannabis, through to a very small minority of heroin and crack cocaine users.

In Chapter 2 we look at how drugs availability underpins all these scenes but in particular we describe how the millions of young Britons who have tried or use drugs 'recreationally' actually obtain their supplies. The reality is light years away from the assumptions held by adult worlds.

In Chapter 3 we describe how recreational drug trying and use is developing amongst British youth via a longitudinal study of several thousand young people across their adolescent years. We also challenge the assumption, by describing their actual profiles, that these adolescents are in some way developmentally deviant or at risk. In Chapter 4 we continue this theme by concentrating on qualitative studies showing how and why young people make and remake drugs decisions right across their adolescence into young adulthood. The dynamism and complexity of their cost–benefit decision-making contrasts with the assumptions held in the war on drugs discourse and indeed much school-based drugs prevention.

Chapter 5 looks at how drug use is increasingly found in Britain's young adult and twentysomething population. In particular it describes a large-scale study of the dance drug users who are found in the dance club–nightclub scene. They are at the most serious end of recreational drug use and we thus look particularly carefully at the consequences of their excessive psycho-active weekends, not just for their own health and safety but for governance. The clubbers challenge the State and in particular its commitment to current drugs laws and their enforcement.

In Chapters 6 and 7 we review the underbelly of UK drugs, focusing on more hidden problematic drug use. Chapter 6 explores the impact of a new wave of heroin use affecting Scotland and the English regions. It analyzes the profiles of very young new heroin users and their unhappy careers as they become first heroin and then often poly drug-dependent. We look at why such problematic drug careers are developing beyond the reach of official interventions and highlight the consequences of this neglect. In Chapter 7 we listen to crack cocaine users and describe their drugs journeys and the consequences of these in respect of both personal and community damage. These poly drug careers may not, in theory, be untreatable but in practice we struggle to see how as currently organized and resourced the drugs interventions industry can deliver what is required.

Finally, in Chapter 8 we compare our jigsaw picture of the realities of UK drugs with the government's high profile 'integrated' drugs strategy and its aspirations to radically reduce drugs availability, drug taking and crime related to dependent drug use. The strategy will be sorely stretched by the complexities and dynamism of Britain's drugs landscape and the epidemiological dramas currently unfolding in the new decade. We argue that the new strategy, while a welcome break with the crude war on drugs, remains susceptible to the forces of conservatism and thus a lack of official honesty and open-mindedness. Currently the management of UK Drugs Unlimited also lacks sophistication borne of a dearth of reliable drugs data, an absence of monitoring and forecasting procedures and grossly inadequate policy delivery mechanisms. In the end full attention will be given to all this because, as we show, the UK drugs landscape will remain challenging for many years to come. Our book tries to show how and why drugs policy in Britain needs to catch up with drugs realities.

1
Unbelievable? The UK's Drugs Present

Howard Parker

Purpose

The UK has an exceptionally drug involved population. This chapter demonstrates this by comparing drug use, especially 'recreational' use involving young people, with North American and European prevalence rates. During the 1990s Britain saw widespread problematic heroin use develop in many of its poor communities for the first time. Out of this its drugs interventions industry began to develop especially around treatment regimes and harm reduction programmes. These early developments are summarised.

Straight on the heels of its first heroin epidemic the UK saw an unprecedented expansion in young people's recreational drug trying. This growth continued across the 1990s to the extent that the normalisation of recreational drug use is probably the best conceptual explanation. However a key question posed here is what will happen as drugwise, drug experienced children of the 1990s become young adult citizens in the new millennium? Will they carry their drug use, mainly of cannabis and the dance drugs with them as 'twentysomethings'?

In response to all this the UK began to develop a drug strategy. The first attempt to formalise this began in the early 1990s. It was strong on war on drugs rhetoric and weak in all other respects. However at the new millennium there is a new more coherent, well resourced strategy with ambitious targets to prevent and reduce drug use and associated problems. This chapter thus sets up the conundrum: how effectively will the new approach deal with the realities and complexities of UK drugs?

The Comparative Picture

The UK now has the most drug experienced population in Europe. In excess of three million young people (16–29 years) in the UK use an illicit drug at least once each year even based on conservative extrapolations from household surveys. In respect of young people's drug use (15–16 years) each of the four UK countries has higher rates than any other 25 European states. Using a standardised school based survey technique overall 40 per cent of those surveyed in the UK had tried at least one drug (Scotland 50.1 per cent, England 39.6 per cent, Wales 32.1 per cent, Northern Ireland 18.4 per cent). Only nearby Ireland (37 per cent) came anywhere near this level with the European norm being around 10 per cent (ESPAD, 1997). These stark drugs realities are confirmed by each comparative study which has been undertaken during the 1990s.

A European Union funded investigation into 'synthetic' drug use (amphetamines, ecstasy and LSD) across the Union, based on mid-90s data taken from school based surveys, national survey findings and seizure and treatment data, unequivocally placed the UK not only at the top of the league table for lifetime and regular use of these drugs but at several times the rates of the 12 member states analyzed. Where rates of ecstasy use were at 8.3 per cent for British 15–16 year olds the norm was around 3 per cent; for amphetamines where 13.4 per cent of British adolescents reported experience of this drug the mean was under 5 per cent and the same picture was generated for LSD. Using household surveys for these drugs, the UK lifetime and past year percentages for adult populations are again several times higher than the mean and no other countries had rates approaching those of the UK (Griffiths *et al.*, 1997). This picture is generally confirmed in the annual monitoring reports produced by the EU (for example, EMCDDA, 1999).

Historically the UK looked across the Atlantic for signs of things to come drugwise. It was widely believed through the 1990s that the USA had both far higher rates of illicit drug involvement and also bred particularly serious drugs problems. Certainly heroin history supported this view, however, methamphetamine and crack cocaine have not become 'global' in the same way. Indeed although ecstasy use originated in the States young Britons are today more likely to use dance drugs than their American peers. Thus in reality the picture is far more complex.

Most importantly the UK has now 'caught up' the USA. When we compare the main American indicators, such as the *National Household Survey on Drug Abuse* or the *Monitoring the Future* surveys of students, we find very similar figures to those generated by similar methods in the

UK. Although the different educational grades/year groups used by the two educational systems makes exact comparisons difficult, the key conclusion must be that only a few percentage points now separate the drug involvement of youth/young adults in the two countries. There are differences by drugs preference and there are specific age cohorts in both countries which have particularly high rates of drug involvement and which can be seen 'running through' time series surveys. However when we look at the overall picture the most marked feature is similarity. The UK enters the new decade with roughly the same scale of drug involvement as the USA and, indeed, with the possibility that unless trends change it will overtake the States in respect of recreational drug use.

It is not clear why the British have become such a drug involved population. While the rates of alcohol and tobacco use are on the high side in comparative analyses across Europe, it is only with illicit drugs that they are many percentage points ahead. It is interesting that Ireland comes closer to the UK drugs profile than any other European country but there is no authoritative literature which attempts to explain this extraordinary status and surprisingly no authoritative Anglo-American thesis either.

We do not attempt such an ambitious explanation but instead we describe and explore how the UK has become so drug involved and try to demystify current drugs realities. We begin by reviewing recent drugs history, remembering all the time that prerequisites to increased use are increased supply, distribution and availability near the point of consumption (see Chapter 2). As we do this, we will refer to landmark developments in drugs policy and practice. Prior to the 1980s, drugs policy was led by the Home Office and was in truth an esoteric footnote of government. It orbited around the 1971 Misuse of Drugs Act, knee-jerk responses to occasional popular drugs fashions and finding better ways to manage a tiny, largely London based, heroin using population. Twenty years on we find drugs policy has a place at the heart of government and with elaborate co-ordination and delivery systems to manage a growing drugs interventions industry whereby almost every health, welfare, care and control and enforcement official is expected to play a role in a local multi-agency partnership approach to dealing with drugs.

We break into the UK's drugs history at the end of the 1970s setting aside discussion of earlier times and drugs scenes from speeding mods to tripping hippies – which were essentially subcultural, temporary drugs fashions. While remembering that recreational drug use was growing and diversifying during the 1980s, the most significant drugs arena revolved around heroin. That it was only such a small number of heroin users, perhaps 100 000 (in a population of over 55 million) who were the 'victims' of the UK's first heroin epidemic but who in turn generated a major drugs problem which adversely affected many others, is itself salutary.

The UK's First Heroin 'Cycle'

At the beginning of the 1980s, the UK, although Northern Ireland was unaffected, experienced its first substantive heroin outbreaks. Although small networks of heroin users, primarily London based, were around prior to this and localised 'outbreaks' did occur (De Alceron, 1969), these were rare.

The new heroin users were young (18–25 years), initially primarily male and came from deprived urban environments. These heroin users (Parker *et al.*, 1988; Pearson, 1987) were basically poor, undereducated, unemployed, 'marginalised' young men. Heroin outbreaks centred on Merseyside (Parker *et al.*, 1988; Fazey, 1987), Greater Manchester, Glasgow (Haw, 1985), Edinburgh, parts of London (Hartnoll *et al.*, 1985) and, to a lesser extent, Bristol (Gay *et al.*, 1985). By the mid 1980s these outbreaks had spread to other towns and cities but primarily on the west side of the Pennines and down into Wales (Bloor and Wood, 1998) rather than the east side of the British Isles.

Drug related crime

It is perhaps common-sense that if heroin use is found – as it is – primarily in poor communities and in turn among alienated young men with poor educational and occupational prospects, then they will turn to acquisitive or petty crime to fund their habits. However the UK studies undertaken at the time managed to paint a more sophisticated picture (for example Hammersley and Morrison, 1987; Parker and Newcombe, 1987). First, when we profile those who are both acquisitive offenders and heroin users we find that only a minority were drawn into crime for the first time by heroin bills (Parker *et al.*, 1988). The majority however had delinquent careers *before* they became dependent on heroin. Their drug use merely amplified their criminal careers and focused them on instrumental acquisitive offences such as shoplifting, theft from vehicles, robbery and burglary. It also made them commit these crimes with greater regularity and less caution.

However, this relationship should not be exaggerated. State benefits support drug habits along with cash in hand from occasional work, drug dealing and, for women, working in the sex industry. While 'deviant', these methods of obtaining funds for heroin or crack cocaine do not significantly ratchet up local crime figures (ISDD, 1994).

Personal and public health problems

By the end of the 1980s we were able to see just how destructive and costly these outbreaks had been on personal and public health. While pure heroin in moderate doses is not particularly associated with ill health, the 'smack' or 'junkie' lifestyle is. Living in poverty, in sink housing, not prioritising resources for diet or personal care, in time produces numerous personal health problems. Many of these – poor skin tone, weight loss, rotten teeth, abscesses – become the hallmark of the junkie image which, alongside 'out of it' weird behaviour, also create a stigma which many users suffer from. The switch to injecting as well as producing personal health problems, particularly damage to injection sites, was also related to hepatitis and, most importantly, the transmission of the HIV virus through equipment sharing and unsafe sex. This often occurs within the sex industry where female dependent users sometimes operate to support their habit.

We should set these morbidity measures in the wider context of 'family' life. Young dependent heroin users often have to break off relationships with parents and relatives after endless disputes about theft from within the home and unwanted house calls from unpaid drug dealers (Dorn *et al.*, 1987). Heroin dependent offspring were routinely arrested and spent periods in custody. Gradually many found themselves in 'hard to let' housing, struggling with ill conceived romantic relationships. This in turn raised major child care and child protection issues about whether and when heroin using young adults made good enough parents (Kearney and Ibbetson, 1991; Klenka, 1986).

While we have seen heroin use develop in a particular town or city slowly and incrementally, another lesson from international postwar drugs 'history' is that heroin use has a strong tendency to grow in an *epidemic* fashion. Although there are some dangers in using this term it does succinctly capture the way heroin use spreads rapidly both socially and geographically. This type of drug spread was first fully documented in the USA when a series of full blown, postwar, heroin epidemics affected many American cities. The model developed by Hunt and Chambers (1976) and Hughes (1977) was tested and revised for the UK by Fazey (1987), Parker *et al.* (1988) and Pearson (1987).

Basically heroin epidemics start unnoticed but spread very rapidly. Two processes are at work. *Microdiffusion* involves the spread through personal contact. More experienced users facilitate novices, the 'know-ledge' about price, purity, how to smoke, chase or inject, what feelings to look for and so on, are passed on between associates and friendship networks. In a full blown epidemic this diffusion occurs simultaneously on numerous sites. Thus density is increased as the results of micro-diffusion join up initially, primarily, in densely populated urban areas. Over time several heroin sites develop in one town or city but not only do they 'join up' they also, through *macrodiffusion*, spread to neigh-bouring areas. Clearly supplier and dealer movement, to avoid surveil-lance or to open a new market, is one method of macrodiffusion. The migration of users to another 'quieter' area or town is another. Police dispersal of an open market or 'junkie' meeting area is, alas, another.

The remarkable thing about this initially American model was its applicability to the UK's heroin outbreaks in the 1980s. Parker *et al.* (1988) undertook a four year study of the heroin epidemic on the Wirral, Merseyside which with a population of 340 000 moved from having almost no heroin users at the beginning of the 1980s to about 4000 six years later. The new cases (incidence) peak over a few years but because few heroin users give up in the short run the number of users in the community at any particular time (prevalence) continues to rise for several years. The consequences for communities hosting a heroin out-break thus last many years, and at enormous social and economic cost, as Britain discovered during this first cycle. This heroin epidemiology, as we shall see (Chapter 6), is of more than historical interest as the new decade unfolds.

Official response lessons

During this heroin dominated period and particularly because of the fear of HIV/AIDs transmission through unsafe injecting practices, the foundations of current drugs services were laid. Most urban conurba-tions developed community alcohol and drugs services or community drugs teams (CDTs).

The basic ingredients were a part-time psychiatrist and a range of drugs workers, predominantly community psychiatric nurses, social workers, probation officers, outreach workers, counsellors and ex-users. However these services were very basic, having only minimal access to detoxification schemes and rehabilitation programmes; they revolved around methadone. Initially in many areas methadone was seen as a community based detoxification tool but it has gradually become increas-ingly utilised for long term 'maintenance' regimes, whereby presenting heroin users were given oral methadone as a substitute for their street heroin. In terms of stabilising local heroin populations, reducing their acquisitive crime rates and use of street drugs, these programmes have been largely successful (Hough, 1996; Parker and Kirby, 1996). Moreover in the midst of public panic about the spread of the HIV virus a major programme of secondary prevention – harm reduction initiatives – was sanctioned. The only time problem drug users became a group the state wanted contact with! Again these initiatives were successful, and by and large HIV spread was quickly brought under control and especially among injecting drug users (McKeganey and Barnard, 1992). The UK still maintains an unusually low rate of HIV positive citizens including injecting drug users.

Although a 'heroin screws you up' public advertising campaign had mixed results, many lessons for future drugs policy emerged during the 1980s. First, it became clear that a very small population of problem drug users, in this case heroin – chasers–injectors, can cause great harm to themselves, their families and, through drug dealing, prostitution and especially crime, to their communities. Second, there was an identifiable life cycle to these heroin outbreaks of around ten years. Third, it was shown that secondary prevention – harm reduction initiatives – can be very effective management tools especially in respect of public health goals. Fourth, it certainly seemed reasonable, at the time, to conclude that the treatment sector through methadone regimes could deal reasonably effectively with the heroin dependent population.

What didn't emerge as a political priority was a commitment to maintain and modernise the treatment sector to deal with future problematic drugs arenas. Perhaps part of the reason for this was the false alarm over crack cocaine. Given that the wisdom at the time was that the UK follows America, but several years behind in respect of drugs problems, dire warnings from the USA (Stutman, 1989) that a crack cocaine epidemic would soon hit Europe and the UK, were taken very seriously. A research hunt for crack cocaine users was quickly mounted, but while crack takers were found in small numbers and particularly in heavy end scenes and the sex industry, no epidemic spread was identified (Stimson *et al.*, 1993).

The non penetration of crack cocaine and settling of the heroin problem meant the media and, thus politicians, turned to other '1990s' drugs stories. The drugs treatment sector dropped down the pecking order in terms of funding and investment. This sector left the 1980s with no training or qualification route for its workforce. Many projects had insecure funding, there was no quality assurance system and no comprehensive developmental template to guide local funders. The most important point to make is that at the end of the 1990s, as we shall see, nothing has changed. The treatment sector has not been professionalised, modernised or encouraged to diversify its treatment options beyond methadone. It is still not quality assured. This indifference by recent consecutive Conservative administrations is a classic example of a lack of accountability in government whereby the price of negligence is only paid many years later – as it happens, by an ambitious Labour administration.

In Chapters 6 and 7 we will discuss this price as we describe what are the beginnings of a second heroin cycle alongside the gradual spread of cocaine and crack cocaine use. It may well be the development of a second highly problematic period based around these drugs which will finally highlight the unlearnt lessons.

The 1990s and the Normalisation of Recreational Drug Use

It is likely that we will look back on the 1990s as a watershed decade in respect of illicit drug use. On the one hand 1988–98 has already been dubbed the 'decade of dance' to crystallise the fusion of ecstasy and the dance drugs with a certain style of music and clubbing (see Chapter 5). On the other hand it was the decade when young people's drug use became a fascination for the media and an outrage for the war on drugs warriors. The league topping status for drug use referred to earlier was created during the 1990s and was generated by very young Britons to the genuine shock of their elders. We have elsewhere referred to this as the process of normalisation of adolescent drug use (Parker *et al.*, 1998). Although we will outline this conceptualisation, other ways of describing these changes are available in terms of increased availability of street drugs, massive increases in drugs trying, an increase in regular recreational drug use, the blurring of the licit (for example alcohol) with the illicit (for example cannabis) and the reluctant social acceptance of sensible drug use by non drug users among British youth, whereby, opinion surveys suggest that the majority would welcome or accept some decriminalisation of cannabis possession.

Normalisation is a social as well as behavioural process and so we can measure it on several dimensions. Tobacco use was normalised for most of the last century and not in age or class specific sectors. However at the new millennium there are clear signs of objection to its use as health risks and the pollution of public space become more salient. Thus, tolerance by non smokers has reduced and smokers are being increasingly stigmatized and segregated. Normalisation is always, at least theoretically, a two way street.

During the 1990s the use of cannabis in particular and other stimulant drugs, to a lesser extent, has become normalised, certainly in the under 30 age group on all the above measures. First, the availability of street drugs has increased enormously, probably tenfold (Cabinet Office, 1999). Young people report early, easy access to most street drugs in nearly all the confidential self report surveys of the 1990s. Second, drug trying rates now stand, depending on region and research method, at 50–65 per cent for under 25s. While sensitive self report surveys find over 60 per cent of young people even in their teenage years have tried one or more street drugs (for example Barnard *et al.*, 1996; Meikle *et al.*, 1996; Parker *et al.*, 1998), even household surveys now find the majority of young Britons have tried illicit drugs. The British Crime Survey for instance has over the past three biannual audits shown (for 16–24 year olds) increases from 45 per cent (1994) to 48 per cent (1996) to 52 per cent (1998) with the figure for young men now at 58 per cent (Ramsay and Partridge, 1999). Those who have never tried a drug are now in a minority.

On more recent regular use there are also signs of increases, whereby, in detailed longitudinal studies we find over a quarter are regular drug users (primarily of cannabis, followed by amphetamines) at the end of adolescence (Parker *et al.*, 1998). The household surveys find roughly one in five past month users and one in four past three month users (for example HEA, 1999).

While there are signs of twentysomething drug use increasing it may well be that regular recreational drug use will not grow much further, whereby, we should not expect more than a quarter of the young adult twentysomething population to take up regular use. However, normalisation does not require 'everyone' to be taking drugs, as with tobacco we do not have a situation where most citizens are regular smokers but we have, for many decades, had coexistence and accommodation of smokers by non smokers. It is here with social and cultural accommodation of certain styles of illicit drug use that we must carefully assess normalisation. Do drug users and non users coexist, tolerate each other, mix socially, co-habit and so on? Most empirical studies conducted during the 1990s (see Chapter 3) suggest this is becoming the case, not in early adolescence and not in today's middle aged but in the say 16–30s age range – the 'going out' age groups (see Boys *et al.*, 1998; Makhoul *et al.*, 1998; Measham *et al.*, 2000; Perri 6, 1997). A key question for the new decade is whether young people will carry over this tolerance (Pirie and Worcester, 1999) of recreational drug use into their adult years and thus extend normalisation across the age range. We will refer to this issue throughout the book.

Waging War on Drugs Together

The UK government's strategic response to all this drug involvement and associated blame and worry about young people's drug use was to develop a national strategy. *Tackling Drugs Together* (HMSO, 1994), which aside from some minor differences between the four countries, applied to the whole UK. It was a strange mix that was launched by John Major the then prime minister. It called for a new partnership approach to dealing with drugs. The most tangible feature of this was the creation of Drug Action Teams (Drug Co-ordination Teams in Northern Ireland). These were to bring the key players together at the local level. Senior representatives from the police, health, education, social services, probation, drug services, voluntary and community organisations and so on, were to produce a corporate strategy for each local area across the UK. This new structure was to identify local problems, share information and produce multi-agency responses with clear objectives and on-going monitoring. For many this was a strategy laden with irony given the track record of the government at the time for being demonstrably unjoined-up and short-termist.

The other main feature of this outline strategy was its misconceptions and misinformation role. It was loaded with war on drugs rhetoric. First, all young people were 'at risk of drug abuse' because of peer group pressure to take drugs. Second, all (illegal) drugs are bad and dangerous and a menace. Third, because, with no distinctions, drug abuse leads to crime then local communities are also 'at risk' from all drug users. John Major was happy to link *Tackling Drugs Together* with the new right's law and order ticket and youth blaming speeches, whereby at its launch he claimed 'no single crime prevention measure could be more significant than success on the front against drugs' (Social Market Foundation, 9 September 1994).

In fairness this war rhetoric was exactly that because the Conservative government did not develop any coherent programmes aimed at real drug using offenders although it did invest in a Drugs Prevention Initiative (DPI). The DPI was intended to develop drugs prevention programmes and identify templates for good practice to be taken up by the Drug Action Teams and secondary schools. Nothing of substance flowed from this strategy of the mid 1990s in respect of modernising the treatment sector.

New Labour's Drugs Strategy (1998–2008)

The change in government in 1997 brought in a New Labour administration, which having spent 17 years in opposition, had plenty of time to work on its own drugs strategy. *Tackling Drugs To Build A Better Britain* (Cabinet Office, 1998) is far better than its title would suggest, though whether it will survive for a decade is a moot point.

Again there are subtle differences in approach and language for each country (for example *Scotland Action In Partnership* (The Scottish Office, 1998); *Drug Strategy for Northern Ireland* (Northern Ireland Drugs Campaign, 1999) but essentially there is one UK approach. The war on drugs rhetoric has largely gone although nanny statements about healthy lifestyles and personal potential are abundant. This said, peer pressure remains a quoted reason for drug use which must be 'resisted'.

In general, however, the strategy is more pragmatic about the current situation than any previous statements and covertly introduces a switch away from faith in crude enforcement towards both prevention and – for the casualties – one-to-one treatment. Indeed of the strategy's four key goals 'to stifle availability of drugs on our streets' is the least developed and has few explicit targets. There is a tacit agreement in the strategy documents and first Annual Report (Cabinet Office, 1999) that the tenfold increase (1987–97) in the amount of drugs seized, number of individual seizures and offenders dealt with is indicative of increased supply and availability rather than enforcement success. This is a brave break with the spin a war on drugs discourse would utilise, but by implication it puts even greater pressure on the other three goals and particularly the centrepiece 'to help young people resist drug misuse to achieve their full potential in society'. Given the quoted drug use reduction targets attached to this goal, this is, as we shall see, an ambitious aim.

The other two key goals mark a shift from an overt to a more subtle law and order approach. Hope and significant resource investment is now pinned on identifying drug driven or drug related offending in the criminal justice system (Edmonds *et al.*, 1999; Turnbull, 1999). Thus a shift from crime reduction through enforcement to coercive (not compulsory) treatment is evident, whereby the goal of providing treatment is 'to enable people with drugs problems to overcome them and live healthy and crime free lives'. The achievement of this goal would simultaneously facilitate the delivery of the final goal 'to protect our communities from drug related anti-social and criminal behaviour'. The key to achieving this related goal is pinned on detecting problem drug users within the arrestees population and 'treatment and testing' orders being made by sentencers and/or prisons providing drug treatment programmes with perhaps compulsory urine testing of arrestees as well. This however requires a major expansion in an already stretched treatment sector.

By creating a Drugs Tsar and a Cabinet Office team, the UK Anti-Drugs Co-ordination Unit, to try and link up government thinking and action, and utilize the Drug Action Team structure to deliver progress on each of the four key goals and attendant performance indicators, New Labour set out its stall early in its term. In copying the USA and including transparent targets the government has been either brave or foolhardy or both. In Chapter 8 we will reflect further on whether this strategy is likely to deliver or indeed survive given the way the politics of re-election and short term imperatives have a strong tendency to undermine long-term strategy.

Conclusion

The UK now has the most drug involved population in Europe and joins the USA in leading the international post-industrialised drug taking league tables. Most of this is recreational drug use by adolescent and young adult populations although the heavy end heroin–cocaine situation is deteriorating.

For some, mainly over 35 year olds and especially parents of teenagers and community elders, this is 'unbelievable'. They have seen, heard and absorbed the media's treatment of the drug problem throughout the 1990s and most are genuinely fearful for young people, believing that drug trying is very risky, health damaging, likely to lead to addiction and entangle the user in criminal worlds. The highlighting of drug related deaths among young drug users, especially in respect of ecstasy and in Scotland, heroin, only reinforces their notions of the dangers of drug use. Having very little knowledge about different drugs and their effects or of why drugs accidents occur and how they can be minimized, they are genuine supporters of the war on drugs. All drugs are bad and dangerous. Thus any drugs strategy which claims not to be going 'soft' but instead promises to deliver supply reduction through enforcement, educate young people to resist drug use even from the early years, make communities safer by reducing drug related crime and provide treatment for the addicted user, will have widespread public support. Political parties know this.

New Labour's response promises all of this. The new ten year strategy (1998–2008) has an unprecedented coherence and transparency and is being backed by around £250 million new money in the first five years. However at the millennium there are plenty of challenges ahead for this strategy. With drugs availability stronger than ever, over half of young Britons having tried a drug and around one-in-five being recreational drug users, the trends are upward. A focus on heroin and cocaine, how-ever pertinent, will make aspirational goals particularly hard to achieve. Moreover the drugs treatment sector is looking sorely stretched even before new demands must be met.

We will address the prospects for this new strategy as we present our cameos of the British drugs landscape. We do this by trying to draw out the realities of different drugs arenas and types of users and identify what the best management of each might look like. This is a complex task but it demonstrates a key point that this is how drugs realities are – complex, often counter intuitive, even contradictory. Thus dealing with drugs should not remain locked in a moral paradigm, it must be based on empirical and cultural realities and so become sophisticated and dynamic. Throughout this collection we also elude to the UK's drugs futures and in Chapter 8 we argue that through epidemiological and social modelling we can produce drugs forecasts. Such an approach has been dismissed by government across the 1990s because the state appar-atus is preoccupied with chasing the latest 'problem' or attempting to demonstrate success in previously declared goals.

Finally the politicisation of drug use/misuse means that we must include all these political and public discourses about drugs, how the UK thinks, talks about and responds to illegal drug use, in the whole equation. We must look not just for intended but unintended conse-quences, for example the switch from ecstasy to cocaine among young recreational drug users, because war was declared on ecstasy, skewing young people's perceptions of the relative dangers of stimulant drugs. Essentially we ask why the UK, given that it has had a relatively sophist-icated drugs interventions industry, actively engaged in education and prevention, enforcement and treatment, has been despite all efforts and annual expenditure of £1.3 billion (Cabinet Office, 1998), so patently unsuccessful in its war on drugs.

2
Unenforceable? How Young Britons Obtain Their Drugs

Howard Parker

Purpose

In this chapter we look at how young people who try and use drugs actually obtain them. The normalisation of adolescent recreational drug use and the increases in drug use by young adults means most young Britons who use drugs are 'normative': nearly half are women, a high proportion are from conventional homes, many are becoming 'responsible' citizens. Most have no wish to come into personal contact with 'real' drug dealers and expose themselves to 'risks' in respect of trouble in criminal worlds, getting caught or buying 'dodgy gear'.

Talk of drug dealers hanging around the school gates seems bizarre once we explore how young people actually obtain their drugs. We find that the main recreational drugs are, near the point of consumption, primarily distributed by young people themselves. They 'sort' each other using their friendship and acquaintance networks whereby the classic source is 'a friend of a friend'. The definitions of possession and supply, of user and dealer, blur. In turn the goal of stemming the availability of street drugs to young people becomes highly problematic. However, the consequent dilemmas involved in criminalising thousands of otherwise largely conforming young people, which this social reality triggers, are largely academic because the social arrangements guarding these transactions are highly effective. Even if the state wished to utilise the law on drugs supply near the point of consumption the scale of resources required and unintended consequences which would flow would be so great as to make the strategy unenforceable.

Strong Supply and Availability

One of the prerequisites for sustaining populations of illicit drug users is supply and availability. We do not fully understand why availability of such a wide range of drugs should have developed in the UK. Clearly once a country develops its drugs habit and demand remains high, then it will become a targeted market because sales will be strong and internal distribution sophisticated. How this process was developed is unclear but the current reality is that the UK now 'receives' a disproportionate share of the drugs business which is estimated to be 8 per cent of all trade (Cabinet Office, 1999). This growth in supply and availability is increasingly acknowledged by the British government, whereby, statements like 'between 1987 and 1997 there has been a tenfold increase in the amount of drugs seized, number of seizures and number of offenders dealt with' (Cabinet Office, 1999) are no longer hailed as a sign of success. Because prices have fallen but 'purity' levels remained stable and rates of drug use risen, seizure rates are almost certainly a measure of the massive amounts of drugs entering the UK.

We thus have private realism among enforcement agencies, but as ever political rhetoric and naivety about 'stemming the tide' by locking up drug dealers who stand outside the school gates, and so on. A good example of this dissonance occurred in 1999 when the British Parliament launched an enquiry (Committee of Public Accounts, 1999) into supply control. Customs and Excise were accused by Members of Parliament (MPs) of appearing 'to be fighting the war against drug smuggling blindfold, with inadequate information about the scale of the task or the impact of their action'. The enquiry was also bemused by Customs and Excise arguing that, first, it had sufficient resources and second it did not believe that attempting to quantify the size of drugs market would help. In this case the enforcement managers' realism was pitted against the politicians' naivety or games playing. This is one of the greatest handicaps to developing a realistic drugs strategy: the war on drugs discourse demands the impossible rather than the feasible and thus fails to deliver either.

Even if supply enforcement had been the primary target in the new strategy it would have been undermined by cost, both directly to the Treasury and indirectly in respect of the legitimate economy. The drugs trade has a symbiotic and parasitic relationship with the legitimate economy but the political and public demand to control the drugs 'problem' is never likely to ever challenge the ultimate priority – to maximize efficient international trade and trading relationships in order to maintain economic growth and stability. Thus as transport routes by air, sea, rail and road become more sophisticated and carry more passengers and freight, and as international frontiers are removed across the European Union, then so too, if demand for drugs is there or can be created, will drugs trafficking be wholly sustainable. It is simply not a realistic goal either to stem the flow of drugs into the UK nor break up distribution networks and in truth there is only a moderate attempt being mounted so to do because privately government officials, if not their political masters, recognise the impossibility of the task.

In this chapter we move to the point of consumption in respect of drugs distribution and look at how the primary consumers – young people who use drugs recreationally – obtain their supplies of cannabis, amphetamines, LSD, ecstasy and cocaine. We thus explore the question as to how generally conforming non delinquent young people (as described in Chapters 1, 3 and 4) obtain their street drugs, given as we shall see, they have no wish to meet or even transact with 'real' drug dealers. What we discover is that the most difficult market to reach and supply – non dependent and non criminal young drug users – actually undertake the delivery, at the point of consumption, themselves.

Methods

This chapter is based on recent and on-going research undertaken at SPARC. All five studies used to glean data thus describe the contemporary situation in England and are further utilised elsewhere in this collection.

1. The North West Longitudinal Study* was a five year investigation (1991–96) into the role of alcohol and illicit drugs among 700, eventually 500, 14–18 year olds in two regions of urban-suburban north west England. The data collection involved five annual, confidential self report questionnaires and interviews with 86 of the cohort in Year 4 when they were 17 years old plus several 'critical incidents' case studies (for example, of a panel member being caught by the police in a drug dealer's house). The data used here come from the interviews (see Parker *et al.*, 1998a for full discussion of the methodology). [Funded by the Alcohol Education and Research Council and the Economic and Social Research Council.]
2. The Integrated Prevention Programme Evaluation** is a four year investigation whereby over 3000 young people (13–16 years, 15–18 years) are being tracked by annual, confidential self report questionnaires

exploring their use of alcohol and drugs in the context of their life-styles. A small cohort (n = 27 but finally n = 19) of initially 15 year olds from the panel were interviewed in-depth three times between 1996 and 1998 by the same interviewers. The data from these structured conversations are utilized in this chapter (see also Measham *et al.*, 1998).

3. The Dance Drugs, Nightclubs Study< is a two year study into the health and safety of clubbers and involved 21 nights fieldwork in three nightclubs in north west England. Brief interviews, using a team of eight interviewers, were undertaken with over 2000 customers and nearly 300 in-depth interviews (including voluntary urine samples and temperature, pulse and intoxication monitoring over several hours) were conducted, as well as extensive observational work and conversations with club security, bar staff and so on. The data used in this chapter are extracted from the in-depth interviews which were coded and quantified using SPSS. [Funded by the Economic and Social Research Council.]

4. New Young Heroin Users in England and Wales> was basically a rapid audit of the spread patterns and profiles of a new cycle of heroin outbreaks affecting numerous small cities and towns in specific regions. A survey of all Drug Action Teams (inter-professional local networks) and Police Forces, generating over 200 returns, was supplemented by fieldwork visits to new heroin 'hotspots' and interviews with local professionals and young heroin users. This study informs part of the main discussion about dealing patterns (see Parker *et al.*, 1998a). [Funded by the Home Office Police Research Group.]

5. Profiles of New Young Heroin Users in England≫ was undertaken during 1999 and involved interviewing 86 young, new young heroin users in a small city, a large town and two small towns in England. These interviewees spoke in detail about how they obtained their drugs and brief accounts are included here. [Funded by Department of Health/Drugscope.]

All the interviews were conducted directly by SPARC staff and the methodologies employed are discussed in detail in the sources given. Because very few British studies have been undertaken which focus directly on drugs transactions at the point of consumption (but see Edmonds *et al.*, 1996) one of the few feasible ways of, at least outlining the situation, is to collate accounts and descriptions from studies which indirectly or incidentally explore the 'final transaction'. Each of the five investigations above all purposefully collected drug 'dealing' data which are brought together for the first time in this chapter.

Adolescent Recreational Drug Users

The longitudinal studies, particularly the qualitative components, confirm that most young people's drugs initiations (13–17 years) are in social settings where their friends or acquaintances offer, for free, a drug to try. Passing round the spliff is the archetypal example of this. For many drug triers and occasional users this remains their *modus operandi* – only take drugs when they are offered to you and are being used in 'safe' social settings.

> That was pot....I think I was about 13...with my sister and my mates. These lads who had it, we got in with them, they'd been smoking it for a while but it was our first time. (female, 17 yrs, recreational user)*

> I don't buy some so that I can smoke it (by) myself. It's normally just when it's being passed around people that I end up smoking it. So I'm not going out and buying some because I think 'oh I need some'. It's just if somebody's got some then I'll have a bit, but I don't feel the need to have to go out and buy some. (female, 16 yrs, moderate recreational user)**

Beyond these triers and opportunistic occasional users we found young people who rely on drugs provided from within their social worlds. This can be at school.

> I know some guy at school who can get it (cannabis), although he's not a dealer he knows someone who's not a dealer who can get it. [*Reliable quality?*] The quality's not bad, but getting it's a pain in the arse quite frankly....I never think I'll be able to get it in time and if I do I think it'll be rubbish, until I'm stoned, then I realise it's not actually that bad. (male, 17 yrs, cannabis only user)*

More often it is within 'time out' friendship networks where one or more, usually males, become the drug hunters who sort things out taking 'orders' from others. Although an 18 year old female single parent, who was only really able to go out 'dancing' once a week, saw cannabis as a regular relaxant while 'stuck in the 'ouse'.

Just my close friends and my sister, usual crew. Before we go out . . . my mate's got her own house and everyone sits in there. . . . The speed we used to get it off my other sister's mate. But my mate's boyfriend he deals the pot so we get the pot off him and he can also get hold of speed so we mostly get it off him and if he can't get hold of it we try and get it off my sister's mate. (female, 17 yrs, recreational user)*

Not real dealers?

Not being in direct contact with *real* dealers is a key device in the social construction of the responsible, respectable, recreational drug user utilized by many young people. When asked where he got his cannabis and amphetamines, one young man was adamant

Depends, friends normally if I can, if not I'll send a friend to a dealer. [*Ever go to the dealers yourself?*]
No. I've *never* been to a dealer. (male, 18 yrs, recreational user)*

Somehow in this discourse friends and friends of friends who supply drugs are also re-cast positively because they're 'OK' or they sometimes also give you stuff free or they have to take risks and so deserve the little bonus of either an 1/8 of cannabis or a wrap of amphetamines or an E, for their endeavours. There is also a very blurred line here between who is dealer and who is customer. In the north west study the *majority* of regular recreational users in the interview sample agreed they had been on both sides of the transaction when asked if they'd ever 'sorted' other people requiring drugs.

Yes for friends.
[*For profit?*]
No probably just they give me enough for a few spliffs for getting it for them.
[*How often?*]
Once in a while. Just when they can't get it themselves say once in every one month or two months or something. (male, 17 yrs, occasional recreational user)*

[*Like being the middle man you mean?*]
Yes.
[*Which drugs?*]
Trips, pot, speed, tablets.

[*For profit?*]
No, just for my mates.
[*Cost price?*]
No, the lad who I got them off he'll have made a profit.
[*But you didn't?*]
No.
[*Who were you selling to?*]
My mates and my cousin.
[*Strangers?*]
No.
[*How often?*]
Someone might phone me up and say 'can you get us something', one week it might be 3–4 times a week, then it mightn't be for a month or something. (male, 18 yrs, regular, recreational user)*

These networks or chains in the procuring of drugs near the point of consumption overtly 'protect' the majority of young drug takers from direct negotiations with people they regard as 'real' drug dealers. There is thus distance put between higher level suppliers, the local dealer and user and because the intermediaries are 'friends of friends' then the deliverer is 'OK' and part of the straight world and not a 'scally' or 'radgy'. However, because there are so many 'real' low level dealers and user–dealers at the local community level who live ordinary lives and can be approached relatively safely, then this supply chain is refuelled and sustained. One female sixth former in a small suburban town met her supplier simply by being in the local pub with her boyfriend – again creating the social illusion of legitimacy.

It's a dealer we know in the pub round the corner. . . . Any day, any time he's in the pub waiting for you. If he's ill, like he was ill last week, so his brother was there, you just go in and nod to him and he comes out. (female, 18 yrs, cannabis only user)*

With normalisation, as discussed in Chapter 1, we find non drug triers, because they are friends with using peers, might also become involved in these transactions. One young man from the same town went off in a car with friends 'who were buying for their friends'.

Ecstasy, cannabis. Just the most frequent ones. That's all they go in for, it's the two cheapest to be honest. E you only have a tablet a night and cannabis for a fiver (£5). (male, 17 yrs, abstainer)*

Another who'd given up cannabis but kept in with the same friends continued to 'sort' his friends in a fairly risky way.

> I was the one who usually got it for all of them. . . . I still go down for them all. They just give me two quid (each) to go and get it and bring it back. It's about a five minute walk . . . just around the area. . . . If he hasn't got none, I know someone else. (male, 16 yrs, former cannabis user)**

In both the longitudinal studies it was possible to see how with experience and increasing drug wisdom the chain of intermediaries near the point of sale created opportunities to make a profit.

> Once I knew a lad that was selling Es and this girl came up to me and said 'do you know anyone who's selling Es?' so I said 'yes, how many do you want' and she said 'oh two'. So I went and got two and took the money off her £30. I charged her £15 and they were only supposed to be £10. That's about it really. (female, 18 yrs, problem drug user)*

Several experienced drug users became involved in more clear cut dealing for profit but invariably as a second job: an extra opportunistic earner. One young man who left school at 16 worked away from home returning each weekend. He in fact informally bridged two recreational drug using networks some hundreds of miles apart. He occasionally profited from distributing cannabis and LSD 'trips'.

> [*Who for?*]
> Friends up there and I've got it for friends down here as well.
> [*Ever sold for profit?*]
> Yes . . . I bought a quarter and paid £30 for it and I made £15 on it . . . but that was cutting it up and selling it on to different people. (male, 18 yrs, recreational user)*

None of these respondents considered themselves 'real' drugs dealers. They saw their role as facilitative, as 'sorting' or helping out friends and acquaintances.

Becoming real dealers?

A handful of drug users in the longitudinal studies became involved in more purposeful dealing for profit. They were certainly, to their customers, 'real' dealers. One young man whose family lived and survived on a 'tough' estate grew up with drug use and drug dealing around him. Upon leaving school he took a night job working behind the bar of a local nightclub. The doorman dealt (mainly amphetamines and ecstasy) and also had an arrangement to let in a few other dealers. Our respondent and his friend who worked in the club began to sell ecstasy, amphetamines and cannabis with the agreement of the doorman. They quickly built up a good trade and for over a year had numerous repeat customers. To avoid tensions the doorman then limited dealing to himself and these two.

> So we cleaned up with the doorman and said right fine we'll just stick with this (current arrangement) and we'll also send people to you ... but as part of the deal you back us up if any shit comes off, so like he backed us up and we basically cut everyone out and there was just two sets of dealers me and my friend and the doorman.
>
> The only complaints was if we'd had something (amphetamines) for too long, you know we didn't realise it was going off and we'd say OK fair enough and give them a free bag, keep them happy. We weren't going to be out of pocket, if you kept them happy they kept coming back and if you got the really good stuff instead of going to other normal dealers they'd come back to you and then ... their friends would come and if it was like a first timer we'd go 'oh there's half free' and they'd be happy.

However operating in the real world of dealing for profit led them into serious problems both with the police (CID) and a local 'gang' unimpressed by 'trespassers'.

> I think the worse one was about 12 black guys try dragging you out of the car, that's got to be the worst. I was at college and apparently I'm meant to have sold something to this lad, forced him to buy it then I'm meant to have mugged him with a gun and a couple of other things which I didn't know shit-all about ... and all these guys surrounded the car I was in ... 'get out the car otherwise we're gonna shoot you through the window.' The police turned up and everything got sorted.... (male, 17 yrs)*

These near crises and CID in the club watching their numerous transactions led the pair to stop dealing. They had made several thousand pounds but could see that their activities were going to be stopped by either the police or local 'organised' criminals with stakes in the drugs market. The risk of getting caught, one way or the other, was salutary.

However, a minority do and will 'get caught' either at school/college or by the police. Here the two very different perspectives or social constructions of drug use and dealing clash, as adult authority and drug-wise youth engage. Two young women who had taken LSD 'trips' into school regarded the punishment of a week's suspension (but no police involvement triggered) and a ceremonial dressing down as excessive.

> We have the head master shouting and screaming at us saying that we're no good dirty druggies, whatever. I was glad I was suspended for a week, I saw it as a week's holiday. I had to sit in here, I had to cry to get back into the school, I had to put on all the acting. 'Oh I'll never do any drugs again, I'm sorry that I've put you through this, I know it's all wrong.' One of the governors was sat there saying 'you're dicing with death'. I was sat there thinking to myself 'shit, I only had a trip. I was "dicing with death" and I only had a bit of acid'. (female, 15 yrs, problem drug user)**

Their sense of injustice would have been far greater if, as is usually the case, the police were also called in and cautions issued.

> A lass in our school ... was caught selling a deal, like a fiver deal [of cannabis] to one of her pals. But what had happened was her boy-friend deals and she had found a deal in her bag and one of the lasses had said 'well let me buy it off you'. And that's all it was. She wasn't coming in to the school and going 'oh do you want to buy a fiver deal?' and all this. And somebody found out or somebody grassed her up and there were just complete hell. The headmaster, the police, the parents, everything was totally bang on to her. It was totally bad. (female, 16 yrs, recreational user)**

Functions of recreational drug users' networks

In adolescence most recreational drug taking is a social event, the effects of the drug interact with the social setting to usually enhance the enjoyment of the episode. Such networks of triers and users also tend to provide a relatively safe environment for trying drugs and also, through conversation and the swapping of drugs stories, upgrade the drug wisdom of each young person, helping them apply a cost–benefit assessment as to what drugs to take/avoid and what strategies should be utilized to stay safe. These networks also allow conventional young people to acquire illegal drugs with little risk of apprehension save the 'chance' discoveries of illegal drugs transactions at home, school or in everyday public space. Not having to meet 'real' dealers or take risks in alien environments is another key function of these drugwise friend-ship networks.

There are also weaknesses in these apparently drugwise networks which, as we shall see in later chapters, are being exploited by those wishing to encourage young recreational drug users to take up more addictive and expensive substances – cocaine and heroin.

The Dance Club–Dance Drug Scene

Moving beyond adolescents into the mainly young adult nightclub-dance club scene we find a particularly outgoing sector of serious recre-ational drug users. In the SPARC night clubs study (see Chapter 5) drugs bills for the main sample (n = 330) were routinely between £20 and £100 for a psycho-active night out. These clubbers are immensely drug experienced and if there is a group of recreational drug users who one would expect to utilize drug dealers this is it.

During the 1990s public discourses about ecstasy deaths, all night raves and 'dangerous' nightclubs have focused on nightclub dealers, particularly 'bouncers' and security/door staff, believing them to be the main suppliers to clubbers. Undoubtedly they have real involvement (Morris, 1998) but again this assumption detracts from the reality – that most recreational drug users, including clubbers, are wary of buying drugs from strangers and getting too close to heavy duty characters. In this SPARC study around 20 per cent of clubbers on the interview night got their drugs given to them, for free, by friends, partners and relatives and even of the 70 per cent or so who paid for their drugs for the night out in question only a minority – around 10 per cent – obtained their drugs from unknown dealers and security/bar staff.

Some 60 per cent of the main sample regularly procured their drugs via friends and friends of friends and where dealers were used they were nearly always 'known' regular sources. With 92 per cent disclosing that they have received drugs from friends and 77 per cent agreeing that they have sold drugs to friends – the basic relationships and strategies described for the adolescent recreational scene are repeated. These same informal private negotiations and transactions make successful enforce-ment improbable if not impossible and apprehension is largely a product of carelessness by those procuring drugs or occasional clampdowns on particular clubs.

The public and political discourses about the postmodern nightclub have indeed triggered local clampdowns. Clubs and clubbers suddenly become targets for drugs raids, queue searches and elaborate inspections as the local media or City Hall politics demand action. Clubbers thus take safety precautions. They consume their drugs before queuing or hide them in (usually female) body orifices as further defence mechanisms over and above obtaining them ahead of time from 'safe' sources. Even so this group, because they have been out and about since mid adolescence are netted by routine and 'stop and search' policing of the pub, club, car and street – one-in-five had cautions or convictions under the Misuse of Drugs Act (mainly for cannabis possession).

In conclusion even at the serious end of young adult recreational drug use the consumers play the key role. Their desire to maintain safety in a potentially hazardous arena and to minimize the likelihood of receiving dodgy drugs from dodgy characters continues to shape drugs transactions. The informal friends of friends chain continues to dominate. This type of committed dance drug user clearly comes closer to real dealers and being 'down town' at the weekend patently increases the risk of being caught up in both the drugs economy and reactive 'symbolic' policing. The trick, for them, is to obtain quality drugs and enjoy the night out without contact with either side of the war on drugs – suppliers or enforcers.

Dependent on Drugs, Dependent on Dealers

In Chapters 6 and 7 we discuss the problematic drugs scenes revolving around heroin, crack cocaine and poly drug use. However, the way young heroin users end up procuring their drugs is best discussed here because as regions of the UK become affected by a second cycle of heroin outbreaks we can see how the recreational and 'hard' drug scenes are becoming intertwined and overlapping.

The first heroin cycle was summarized in Chapter 1. After a quiet endemic period (1990–95) signs of a second phase of local outbreaks began to emerge. This time the heroin outbreaks are in small cities and towns, in Scotland and northern and south west England in particular. It is quite clear that these outbreaks are supply led, whereby heroin has become far more widely available and cheaper. Around 20 per cent of 13–16 year olds now report easy access to heroin in these areas – more than a doubling of rates found in the early 1990s (Aldridge *et al.*, 1999). Heroin is now marketed at £10 a bag (about 30 per cent pure 0.1 to 0.08 gm).

SPARC's studies of these young heroin users (see Parker *et al.*, 1998a; Egginton and Parker, 2000) have found that they are introduced to heroin and cocaine through the adolescent recreational scene at around 15 years of age. In other words, while in the midst of the early onset of their drinking, cannabis, amphetamine and tranquilliser trying phase most of the new very young heroin users appearing around the regions are introduced to heroin. Uptake is small involving only a couple of per cent of a local youth population but because of the dire consequences of a heroin career this becomes a growing problem for the communities involved (see also Chapter 6).

One consequence of dependent drug use is that the ways users obtain their drugs changes from the informal and social to the formal and financial. Depending on drug dealers runs parallel to dependency on drugs. The new young heroin users' study found very similar arrangements in four different sites in England. A third of the sample transacted with user dealers or, through time, became user dealers, themselves often 'grafting' for their own higher level supplier. One 17 year old male in a Yorkshire town, once he had become a regular user had an established dealer and 'used to go round to his house for a smoke'.

> When I started to use more I started dealing (for him). I did four months then stopped. (male, 17 yrs, Yorkshire)

But still in debt to his dealer he returned to selling up to 30–40 ten pound deals a day before getting caught and sent to prison.

While user–dealers were likely to be better known to and a similar age as these new young heroin users, their dealing practices were seen as more unpredictable and less reliable both in terms of their availability and quality standards.

> I always get the best deal from non-using dealers. (male, 19 yrs, SW England)

In this world of dependency formal business arrangements take over from the informal sorting of the recreational sites. Of the sample 57 per cent relied on recognised local dealers. Most had a main dealer but knew several others. Most had to telephone through an order then meet at a place nominated by the dealer.

> I ring the dealer up on his mobile and he says where to meet. (male, 16 yrs, NW England)

> A woman (dealer) I phone her and then meet her 'runabout'. Sometimes go to her house but that is only really early in the morning before 8.30am. (male, 16 yrs, NW England)

In this world retailing practices become common particularly when markets are unstable and competition between dealers on-going.

> It changes everyday, all the time. One minute three bags for £25, sometimes even get four bags for £25 . . . depends on the dealer, some do good bags . . . but you can get ripped off. (male, 19 yrs, SW England)

In this world young users meet more and more heavy duty people.

> I met the wrong people, more people selling it, dealers getting caught or ripping people off. (male, 19 yrs, SW England)

> . . . a big dealer moved in and laid people on. (male, 15 yrs, SW England)

These are very different arrangements where 'taxing' for unpaid debt created by lay-ons is always the threat and where being ripped off is common. On the other hand 'real dealers' often work very hard. Our interviewees could either always get heroin 24 hours a day (55 per cent) or at least most times (34 per cent) with only 10 per cent being restricted to set opening times. Over a third (37 per cent) had never experienced a 'drought' and for those that had, while 5 per cent remembered 'panicking' and 'just kept walking', 13 per cent transferred to other dealers, 13 per cent to other neighbourhoods and 7 per cent used substitute drugs to tide them over.

The way problem drug users procure their drugs is consistent with them slipping away from more conventional lives and thus more informal 'careful' ways of obtaining drugs. Both the drugs they use and the amounts they need takes them away from the informal 'sorting' processes into a world of drugs and crime.

Conclusions

There is no doubt that in most British cities and estates in urban areas low level drug dealers operate from their own homes or other residences and receive a stream of calling customers. Indeed intelligence about these dealers is not difficult to obtain hence they are a resource efficient target for local Police Drugs Squads. Nor is there any doubt that young people who get involved in recreational drugs networks can become recognizable drugs suppliers. However, the final section of the distribution chain for the main recreational drugs is found primarily among young drug users themselves. For the vast majority of these young users, uncomfortable with obtaining drugs from 'real' dealers, a highly functional and complex set of social arrangements and transactions have developed. Drugs are obtained for free, from shared purchases and, most of all, from partners, friends and friends of friends. Dealing becomes 'sorting' and sorting, despite money changing hands, is an act of friendship and trust.

Clearly with dependent drug use these arrangements are inadequate and anyway unacceptable to most young recreational drug users who have no truck with heroin and crack cocaine. Thus dependent users and real dealers must and do meet and with all the attendant problems of debt, taxing and intimidation. In Figure 2.1 we offer a very basic spectrum of involvement with drugs and their acquisition. The key point is that the distinctions between 'sensible' recreational drug use and problematic dependent use are reflected in procurement strategies, and the vast bulk of drug users are found in the middle of the spectrum keeping to self imposed rules of engagement which protect them from both sides of the war on drugs: official enforcement and shady criminal worlds.

Even so, with normalisation and hundreds of thousands of young Britons shifting drugs around, between and for each other, then even untargeted, routine policing nets a small minority. With drugs incidents in schools running at many thousands each year (SCODA, 1999) and the everyday policing of youth on the street, in the pub, club and car endlessly discovering small deals, we find cautions for cannabis possession alone rose from 4000 in 1986 to 40 000 in 1996, and still rising steeply, while the number of young people convicted for possession and supply offences also has risen sharply. All this is a consequence of the increasing normalisation of recreational drug use whereby *de jure* we now have a significant minority of young Britons 'guilty' of supply. Sorting friends out with a handful of ecstasy tablets or a gram of cocaine is in fact a serious Class A drugs offence which can and does produce prison sentences. It is as well for the criminal justice system that the Misuse of Drugs Act is as unenforceable as it is in the recreational scene.

Whatever one thinks about this widespread disregard for the Misuse of Drugs Act, one helpful outcome has been that 'sorting' has kept the recreational and harder drugs scenes separate. By not meeting heavy

Have nothing to do with drugs. Keep away from people who do if at all possible.

Remain an 'abstainer' but accommodate drug taking and 'sorting' and sharing among friends and acquaintances.

Take certain drugs, mostly cannabis, but only when they are being used, offered and shared in a safe social setting. Never ask for or attempt to obtain controlled drugs yourself.

Never make a transaction (money for drugs) yourself. Always rely on a partner, friend or friend of a friend's drugs dealer. Ideally 'club' your financial contribution with others.

Only buy drugs from a friend or acquaintance, never a stranger. Only buy certain drugs and never heroin or crack cocaine.

Only buy drugs from a drug dealer you know. Do this because you are drugwise and streetwise and are acting as an intermediary thereby providing a service for friends and acquaintances. As reward your own drugs bill is usually covered.

Only buy drugs from a 'real' dealer exceptionally and then only ones you know.

Be realistic: buy drugs for your (regular) personal use and/or friends by negotiating with one or more established dealers to get best value or credit (lay-ons).

Buy drugs to divide up and sell to cover your own significant drugs bill or to make a profit as well.

Buy drugs, despite the risks, if necessary from any dealer or whoever you can because you need them now.

Figure 2.1 The spectrum: users' rules of engagement with the drugs market

duty drugs dealers from subterranean worlds young recreational drug users have been unlikely to become involved in heroin and crack cocaine.

The unwelcome challenge to this bifurcation is coming from the purposeful supplying of heroin to new markets and potential user populations and the supplying of cocaine powder to recreational scenes focused on stimulant drugs. With such sophisticated distribution systems and so many low level dealers in place it is clearly possible to utilize current social 'sorting' arrangements among recreational drug users to market and supply more dangerous drugs. The vast majority of young people, and indeed most recreational drug users themselves, will still not try nor distribute these drugs (see Chapters 3 and 4), but there is clearly a growing uptake of both heroin (Parker *et al.*, 1998a) and cocaine (Boys *et al.*, 1999; Ramsay and Partridge, 1999) particularly in the 15–30 age groups.

The basic conclusion we reach from all this is that the official goal of 'stifling the availability of illegal drugs on our streets' is not realistically achievable via enforcement. In a global economy and, certainly, once a massive market and diverse distribution system has been created, as in the UK, it is too resource expensive and problematic to stem the supply of drugs. The primary focus on heroin and cocaine (Cabinet Office, 1999) is appropriate but the outcomes are and will be poor. Currently these drugs are now cheaper and more accessible than ever before and we can be fairly confident, utilizing epidemiological knowledge, that the heroin and cocaine markets will remain buoyant at least well into this new decade.

3
Unconventional? Adolescent Drug Triers and Users in England

Roy Egginton, Judith Aldridge and Howard Parker

Purpose

In this chapter we summarise the results of a longitudinal study of nearly 3000 young people in northern England, in respect of their changing drugs 'status' across adolescence. We try to provide a moving picture of how, across adolescence, drugs pathways unfold, thereby, producing the national statistics we outlined in Chapter 1. We also critically examine the assumptions, found primarily in the American literature and taken up by the UK drugs prevention industry, concerning 'at risk' young people. The thrust of this assessment is that those who become regular drug users in late adolescence have personal, social and educational deficits and are at risk of drug 'abuse' as a result. However, do today's British adolescent drug users have these deviant characteristics? Are they 'vulnerable' to poor parenting, low educational attainment and a propensity to delinquency? If they are then notions of normalisation are fragile.

This chapter also offers an innovative approach to measuring regular drug use and distinguishing it from drug trying. Drug *users* must imbibe their drugs fairly frequently and, as importantly, intend to continue to do so. However, very few studies measure frequency of use, instead using 'past month' use as a proxy measure for drug use. Once we begin to unpack the complexities and dynamics of young people's drug pathways through time, we quickly realise how problematic current official assumptions and measuring rods are.

Following on in Chapter 4 we hear the voices of a sub sample of the older cohort talk about their leisure time and the role of alcohol and drugs therein. The rapidly changing rates of drug trying and drug use presented in this chapter take on much greater integrity and meaning if we also understand how they are generated – by most young people continuously making and remaking drugs decisions.

Introduction

The increases in drugs availability and drug trying which have occurred across the 1990s and thus, set the backcloth for this new decade, have been measured primarily by one off 'snapshot' surveys of young people. Most have been undertaken by market research companies on behalf of customers (HEA, 1999) or by school teacher administered surveys (Balding, 1999). Fewer have been undertaken by researchers themselves and without teacher presence. However, whenever they are, rates of disclosure are usually higher (Barnard *et al.*, 1996). Even fewer school based surveys attempt to follow up absentees from the day of administration.

This chapter summarises a study, which was researcher administered, which did follow up absentees and more importantly was longitudinal. It attempted to monitor the same young people over three years and utilized two different age cohorts, in an attempt to monitor drug trying and drug use through adolescence and plot which drugs are involved and how rates of use change across time. We also briefly compare a new young cohort of 13 year olds in 1998 in the same towns and schools with our younger cohort's profile at 13 in 1996.

Finally, the large data set accumulated on these cohorts allows us to compare and contrast the profiles of young drug users with drug triers and abstainers. We look for statistical correlation in respect of 'risk' factors such as family structure, school attainment, religion, ethnicity and so on, to see if there are real differences in the characteristics of those who do take drugs compared with those who don't. In short, are young Britons who take drugs unconventional?

Method

The full methodology for this on-going longitudinal study is described elsewhere (Aldridge *et al.*, 1999) and only a brief, accessible summary is provided here. Table 3.1 describes the three cohorts investigated. This chapter focuses primarily on the younger cohort a who were 13 in 1996 and an older cohort b who were 15 in 1996. Each cohort was surveyed three times. The majority were the same respondents but some of them included in the analysis had missing years, or particularly with the school leavers (year 12 pupils) in 1998, many were lost through attrition. This was because half the older cohort had left school after year

Table 3.1   Northern regions longitudinal study: sampling overview

School year	Year 8	Year 9	Year 10	Year 11	Year 12	Total
Modal age at sweep	13 yrs	14 yrs	15 yrs	16 yrs	17 yrs	
Sweep 1 June 1996	1310[a]		1320[b]			2630
Sweep 2 March 1997		1401[a]		1287[b]		2688
Sweep 3 March 1998	1441[c]		1342[a]		794[b]	3577

a – younger cohort; b – older cohort; c – additional third cohort.

two of the research and had to be surveyed using postal questionnaires. Without funding for incentives such as a music token or voucher, only about half made a return.

These three annual sweep surveys were administered directly by SPARC staff with no teachers present and elaborate processes were involved to guarantee respondents' confidentiality. Whole year groups, initially in a dozen secondary schools, made up the sample. School selection was based on an attempt to create representative samples of these age groups for one town in north east England and two towns in Yorkshire. Absentees were traced and around half completed questionnaires. An analysis of the earlier drugs profiles of those lost showed they were more likely to be drug triers and users. In particular this means the third survey results for the older cohort will reflect under estimations of drug trying and use.

The original questionnaire was extensively piloted. Each year's instrument was specifically designed to focus on young people's drug use, but set within the context of their everyday lives and lifestyles. Over 60 questions explored personal, family and social circumstances, school, delinquency, disposable income, use of leisure time and alcohol and tobacco use. There were also attitudinal questions in respect of different drugs and drug taking behaviour and each respondent's future intentions concerning drug taking were documented.

Alcohol and Tobacco Use

Table 3.2 describes the alcohol and tobacco use patterns in the northern regions' longitudinal sample. These rates are consistent with the national picture outlined in Chapter 1. We found that by early adolescence (13–14 years) nine-out-of-ten have had an alcoholic drink and from around 14–15 years over half are actually weekly drinkers. These rates continue to rise until by age 17 we can see, in the older cohort, over two-thirds are weekly drinkers.

Table 3.2   Alcohol and tobacco use across adolescence

	Younger Cohort (ages 12/13–14/15)			Older Cohort (ages 14/15–16/17)		
	Year 1	*Year 2*	*Year 3*	*Year 1*	*Year 2*	*Year 3*
n size	1310	1401	1342	1320	1287	794
	%	%	%	%	%	%
Ever had alcoholic drink	82.5	88.8	92.6	94.3	95.7	94.1
Weekly drinkers	28.1	50.7	50.0	55.6	68.4	69.6
Current smokers	17.6	25.6	31.9	36.8	40.5	34.8

In respect of tobacco use rates again rise in early to mid adolescence and by 17 years around 40 per cent are smokers (the older cohort suffered school leaver attrition which has artificially deflated the third year rate here). In this study, as across the UK, more young women than young men are smokers. For instance at year two, for the younger cohort when they are 14 years, 21.5 per cent of males were smokers compared to 29.7 per cent of females. In the older cohort, who were aged 16 at that time, 35.1 per cent of males compared to 46 per cent of females were smokers.

Young People's Access to Drugs

The young people in this study have consistently shown very high rates of recognition for all the ten main illicit drugs. Over 90 per cent routinely recognized each drug's name/slang name with many drugs by the third survey attracting almost 100 per cent recognition among both cohorts, particularly for amphetamines, cannabis, cocaine, ecstasy and heroin.

With regard to availability, 43 per cent of the younger cohort at 13 indicated that they had been in offer situations for at least one drug (especially cannabis and solvents) rising to 61 per cent in 1997 and 77 per cent in 1998. By the time these respondents were 15 in our third survey amphetamines (41 per cent), nitrites (40 per cent), magic mushrooms (30 per cent) and ecstasy (25 per cent) were beginning to show high levels of availability although cannabis at 62 per cent was by far the most available drug.

For respondents in the older cohort offer/availability rates for at least one drug were at 72 per cent (1996) rising to 80 per cent (1997) and further to 85 per cent (1998) by the age of 17. In our third survey 76 per cent of this older group had been 'offered' cannabis. There were also high levels of availability for amphetamines (53 per cent), solvents/gases (46 per cent), ecstasy (45 per cent), nitrites (44 per cent) and LSD (41 per cent), as well as worryingly high rates of availability for cocaine at 20 per cent and heroin at 17 per cent.

As we showed in the last chapter getting hold of drugs usually involves opportunism or asking friends and acquaintances to activate the 'sorting' process or nominate a dealer. Particularly in respect of the development of regular drug use this supply process must be reasonably reliable. Table 3.3 shows the ease with which respondents can access different drugs. We asked them if they had the time, inclination and money, how easy/difficult would it be to get each street drug. In summary, solvents, then cannabis and amphetamines were the most accessible for both the older and younger cohorts. Over the three years ecstasy and LSD became more available to the older cohort. Overall, the older cohort always found it easier to access drugs across the three years, however, with heroin and cocaine this difference is very slight. In fact when the younger cohort were surveyed in year three they had easier access to heroin and cocaine than the older cohort had when they were age 16. These findings do not bode well for the UK Drugs Strategy's goal of reducing availability of drugs to young people.

Trying Illicit Drugs

Table 3.4 provides the longitudinal overview of lifetime drug taking for the two cohorts over three annual surveys. Within the younger cohort we can see that even at age 13, 25.6 per cent reported having already tried at least one drug in the first survey, rising through 40.2 per cent to 52.5 per cent by age 15 in the 1998 survey. We can also see significant regional differences with very early onset occurring among respondents from north east England, approximately 61 per cent of whom had already tried at least one drug by age 15 compared to just under half of their Yorkshire contemporaries.

Within the older cohort 51.3 per cent had tried a drug at age 15 rising to 55.9 per cent and again to 57.3 per cent by 17 years of age. Two key points need to be highlighted. First, we see the regional differences fade. This appears to confirm that onset in the north east was genuinely earlier, rather than drug trying being far higher among the region's youth population. Second, we can see in the older group a significant differ-ence between those who stayed on in sixth forms and those who left their secondary schools after GCSEs. Given that almost 65 per cent of 17 year old leavers had ever tried a drug compared with 53.1 per cent of sixth formers and remembering the attrition effect will have almost

Table 3.3 Access to drugs by age cohort, 1996–98

		Younger cohort (ages 12/13–14/15)			Older cohort (ages 14/15–16/17)				
		Survey 1	Survey 2	Survey 3	Survey 1	Survey 2	Survey 3		
							Sixth formers	School leavers	'Year 12' total
n size		1310 (%)	1413 (%)	1342 (%)	1320 (%)	1290 (%)	509 (%)	285 (%)	794 (%)
Amphetamine	easy	37.0	45.6	63.7	66.6	80.1	72.9	76.2	74.1
	difficult	24.4	16.8	12.2	16.2	9.7	8.1	8.3	8.2
	impossible	15.6	7.7	4.6	4.3	1.6	2.8	1.4	2.3
Cannabis	easy	40.5	55.2	74.8	76.3	83.1	85.9	87.0	86.3
	difficult	22.9	12.7	6.6	10.0	4.6	3.4	3.6	3.5
	impossible	15.6	6.9	4.1	3.8	1.7	2.4	0.7	1.8
Cocaine	easy	20.6	22.9	32.3	31.1	31.5	32.7	35.0	33.5
	difficult	33.0	27.4	24.8	34.4	29.1	30.1	23.9	27.9
	impossible	20.3	12.7	8.3	11.8	7.8	7.0	6.6	6.8
Ecstasy	easy	25.1	34.0	44.1	54.9	61.2	61.6	63.0	62.1
	difficult	28.0	21.6	18.9	20.5	15.0	12.7	13.0	12.8
	impossible	20.5	10.9	8.0	6.2	3.5	4.0	0.7	2.9
Heroin	easy	20.3	22.8	30.7	28.7	30.2	30.7	35.2	32.3
	difficult	30.5	26.9	24.9	33.8	31.5	31.7	26.0	29.7
	impossible	21.5	12.7	10.4	12.9	7.4	5.5	5.9	5.6

LSD	easy	28.2	37.7	48.1	58.3	62.8	56.0	61.1	57.8
	difficult	27.0	19.0	14.6	19	13.8	15.1	13.3	14.5
	impossible	18.2	10.4	6.8	4.7	2.6	2.4	2.2	2.4
Magic mushrooms	easy	32.3	40.5	49.5	50.9	55.5	49.7	50.7	50.1
	difficult	26.2	17.0	14.7	22.5	17.0	17.2	16.7	17.0
	impossible	15.5	8.5	6.2	5.0	3.3	4.5	2.2	3.7
Nitrites	easy	29.7	–	54.7	59.3	–	86.9	72.4	61.3
	difficult	24.6	–	11.8	13.8	–	2.5	17.7	10.6
	impossible	19.0	–	5.4	6.2	–	1.6	7.9	2.1
Solvents	easy	65.8	70.9	82.6	86.7	86.3	–	–	87.5
	difficult	9.3	5.4	2.8	3.2	2.1	–	–	2.1
	impossible	8.8	4.3	2.4	2.1	1.1	–	–	1.2
Tranquillisers	easy	32.5	40.3	40.7	50.7	56.5	47.5	54.2	49.9
	difficult	22.4	13.7	14.7	18.8	14.4	15.4	11.2	13.8
	impossible	16.0	7.6	6.8	5.4	1.9	2.1	2.8	2.3
Legal herbal highs'	easy	–	16.0	21.8	–	23.0	26.5	23.5	25.4
	difficult	–	6.4	7.5	–	5.5	6.5	2.1	4.9
	impossible	–	3.1	2.9	–	0.8	1.4	0.4	1.0

Table 3.4 Lifetime trying of at least one drug by age cohort and region 1996–98

Younger cohort (ages 12/13–14/15)	Survey 1			Survey 2			Survey 3		
	NE	Yorks	Tot	NE	Yorks	Tot	NE	Yorks	Tot
n size	462 (%)	848 (%)	1310 (%)	478 (%)	935 (%)	1413 (%)	451 (%)	891 (%)	1342 (%)
Tried at least one drug	34.0	21.1	25.6	51.4	34.4	40.2	60.9	48.3	52.5

Older cohort (ages 14/15–16/17)	Survey 1			Survey 2			Survey 3						
							Sixth formers			School leavers			'Year 12'[a]
	NE	Yorks	Tot	NE	Yorks	Tot	NE	Yorks	Tot	NE	Yorks	Tot	Total
n size	493 (%)	827 (%)	1320 (%)	477 (%)	813 (%)	1290 (%)	126 (%)	383 (%)	509 (%)	122 (%)	163 (%)	285 (%)	794 (%)
Tried at least one drug	57.6	47.4	51.3	60.5	53.3	55.9	48.3	54.5	53.1	62.2	66.9	64.9	57.3

[a] i.e. all the older cohort at Survey 3.

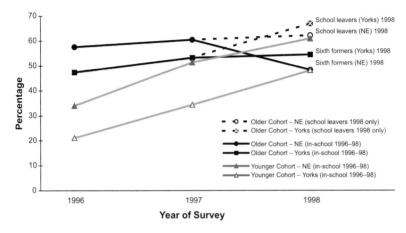

Figure 3.1 Lifetime trying/use of at least one drug by age cohort and region 1996–98 (percentage).

certainly removed particularly drug experienced school leaving panel members, this is an important finding which we will elaborate on in due course.

Figure 3.1 summarises these trends visually across adolescence. We can see there are fairly clear age patterns all suggestive of drug trying rates rising with age but perhaps beginning to plateau at around age 17 old with initiation episodes – the incidence rate – being greater during the mid teens.

Table 3.5 shows the drugs involved in these trying episodes. Cannabis dominates throughout with solvents/gases also being an early initiation drug. Amphetamine trying and nitrite sniffing are also widespread. Notable differences in individual drug use rates are apparent between school leavers and sixth formers in the older cohort, with school leavers reporting substantially higher rates of use for all drugs except legal herbal 'highs'. Early signs of heroin and cocaine uptake can also be seen here given rates of less than 1 per cent have been the norm across the first half of the 1990s.

Past Month Use

Because this chapter is describing different ways of measuring drug *use*, Table 3.6 shows past month prevalence. These past month measures are the main way that regular drug use is estimated in most surveys including the official government measure, the British Crime Survey. For the younger cohort in this study, past month rates of use for at least one

Table 3.5 Individual drugs tried or used by age cohort 1996–98

| | Younger cohort (ages 12/13–14/15) | | | Older cohort (ages 14/15–16/17) | | | | |
| | Survey 1 | Survey 2 | Survey 3 | Survey 1 | Survey 2 | Survey 3 | | |
						Sixth formers	School leavers	'Year 12' total
n size	1310 (%)	1413 (%)	1342 (%)	1320 (%)	1290 (%)	509 (%)	285 (%)	794 (%)
Amphetamines	5.4	9.3	16.5	17.7	20.2	12.8	31.3	19.5
Cannabis	14.6	25.6	42.0	43.6	50.0	46.1	58.9	50.7
Cocaine	1.3	2.0	3.5	2.3	2.2	2.8	3.9	3.2
Ecstasy	1.7	2.8	5.0	5.8	9.7	8.2	15.0	10.6
Heroin	1.1	2.0	3.1	1.6	2.5	1.4	4.0	2.3
LSD	4.6	8.4	11.3	13.9	16.5	8.9	19.7	12.7
Magic mushrooms	5.1	8.8	10.1	10.9	14.3	9.3	11.3	10.0
Nitrites	5.9	16.8	22.7	19.2	27.9	17.2	31.9	22.5
Solvents	13.3	20.2	24.3	18.2	17.8	8.7	15.4	11.1
Tranquillisers	3.0	5.4	8.3	9.2	8.7	4.1	13.4	7.5
Legal herbal 'highs'	–	4.0	4.8	–	5.3	7.1	5.8	6.6
At least one	25.6	40.2	52.5	51.3	55.9	53.1	64.9	57.3

Table 3.6 Past month prevalence for at least one drug by age cohort 1996–98

	Younger cohort (ages 12/13–14/15)			Older cohort (ages 14/15–16/17)				
	Survey 1	Survey 2	Survey 3	Survey 1	Survey 2	Survey 3		
						Sixth formers	School leavers	'Year 12' total
n size	1310 (%)	1413 (%)	1342 (%)	1320 (%)	1290 (%)	509 (%)	285 (%)	794 (%)
At least one drug	10.7	19.5	32.2	28.4	31.7	24.8	32.6	27.6

drug have risen dramatically from 10.7 per cent (1996) to 19.5 per cent (1997) and again to 32.2 per cent (1998). Therefore, in the month preceding the administration of our third survey almost one-third of the younger cohort had taken at least one drug.

Among the older cohort, at 15 years in 1996, 28.4 per cent were past month drug takers rising to 31.7 per cent in the second survey but falling to 27.6 per cent by 17 years, in the third survey. However, this is an artificially low rate, in the final year, due to attrition. Again, importantly, we see that of those who stayed on in sixth form only 24.8 per cent had a past month episode compared to 32.6 per cent of school leavers. This picture seems to confirm both the early onset characteristics in the younger cohort but also that drug trying or taking rates, although still increasing, are doing so less rapidly.

Distinguishing Drug Triers from Users

We know from the other longitudinal study undertaken during the 1990s (Parker *et al.*, 1998) that past month measures in adolescence capture one-off triers and experimenters not just on-going or regular users. This means that utilizing past month rates as a proxy for measuring regular use can lead to over estimation. The key factors in distinguishing *triers* from *users* are regularity of use and future intentions/behaviour in respect of the drug(s) in question. A respondent who discloses smoking cannabis 20 times in the past month is clearly a cannabis user over this period. However recreational drugs careers clearly involve on-going drug use. We expect the use to be maintained at some frequency. Unless our cannabis smoker continues (s)he is no longer a user, rather than an ex-user. A reasonable way of measuring this is to enquire about future intentions. Does the 'user' intend to or expect to continue taking the drug in the future, whereby, the behaviour is ongoing. The most basic way of distinguishing between triers and users is to take past use as a starting point but distinguish between those who expect to take the same or another drug again and those who do not. To this end we have identified four distinctive drug statuses that embrace the whole sample.

Never taken

Those who have never tried an illicit drug and who are often termed abstainers.

Triers/experimenters

Respondents who had a drug at some point in the past but either intended not to have that drug again or had not had the drug again within the past year.

'Potential' users

These respondents had taken a drug within the past year and most importantly for this 'basic' definition intended to do so again.

Regular users

Respondents who have taken a drug at least ten times in the past year, have taken that drug in the past month and expect or intend to continue drug taking.

Table 3.7 shows how these drug statuses have evolved throughout the three surveys and within both age cohorts. There are far less regular users than the traditional 'past month' measure estimates but on the other hand we can see that once a young person has tried a drug she/he is highly likely to do so again.

Concentrating on the 'ever taken a drug' group we can see that 'triers' represent only just over a quarter of this drug experienced sector, whereas basic or potential users make up between 40 and 50 per cent.

Although attrition has meant that the potential and regular drug use rates are under estimates in the older cohort, it is still clear that drug involvement increases with age. This process is particularly apparent in the younger cohort, whereby, potential and regular user rates climb annually. By age 15 around 40 per cent of this sample are actively drug involved, being potential or regular users.

While caution ought to be adopted when interpreting the meaning of such changes in drug status what these measurements do provide are important conceptual distinctions by which triers/experimenters can be

Table 3.7 Drugs trying compared to 'potential' and 'regular' drug use by age cohort 1996–98

Year of survey	Younger cohort (ages 12/13–14/15)			Older cohort (ages 14/15–16/17)				
	1996	1997	1998	1996	1997	1998		
						Sixth formers	School leavers	'Year 12' total
n size	1310 (%)	1413 (%)	1342 (%)	1320 (%)	1290 (%)	509 (%)	285 (%)	794 (%)
Never taken	74.3	59.9	47.6	48.7	44.1	46.9	35.1	42.7
Ever taken	25.7	40.1	52.4	51.3	55.9	53.1	64.9	57.3
Trier/experimenter	9.9	13.9	11.4	12.8	14.6	15.1	19.4	16.6
Potential user	12.8	20.6	26.6	24.7	26.4	23.5	27.6	25.0
Regular user	3.0	5.6	14.4	13.8	14.9	14.5	17.9	15.7
triers/experimenters as % of ever taken	28.5	24.7	21.8	25.0	26.1	28.4	29.9	29.0
potential users as % of ever taken	49.8	51.3	50.7	48.1	47.2	48.6	42.5	43.6
regular users as % of ever taken	11.7	14.0	27.5	26.9	26.7	23.0	27.6	27.4

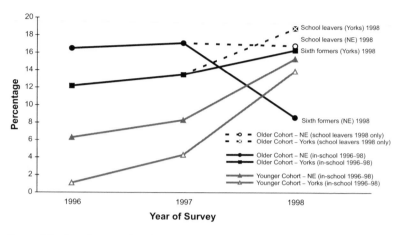

Figure 3.2 Regular use of at least one drug by age cohort and region 1996–98 (percentage).

separated from those who are contemplating further and more regular drug-taking episodes.

Regular Drug Use

Regular drug use encompasses all those who have taken at least one drug in the past month, who expect or intend to do so again, and have also already taken that drug at least ten times in the past year. This now allows us to make accurate calculations as to the proportion of 'regular' drug users in the sample. Moreover this formula becomes a more reliable method for repeated application in other future studies once identical questions have been asked to generate the data.

As Table 3.7 also shows very few 13 and 14 year olds are regular users; only 3.0 per cent. However, by age 15 and 16 this type of use becomes more common; around 14 per cent rising to around 18 per cent among school leavers by age 17. Those staying on in sixth forms are slightly less likely to be regular current users however.

In Figure 3.2 we can also see clear regional differences with Yorkshire sixth formers (16.3 per cent) and school leavers (18.8 per cent) being more likely to be 'regular' drug users than their peers in the north east England. Figure 3.2 also illustrates how the younger cohort in 1998 is already showing signs of being more drug experienced than their elders were when surveyed at the same age in 1996.

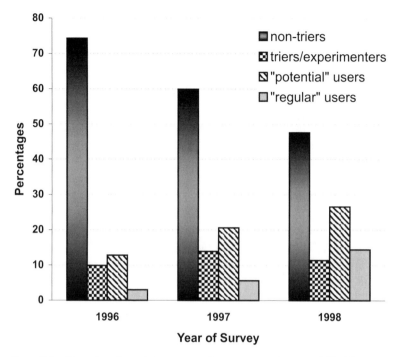

Figure 3.3 Changing drug status among the younger cohort aged 15–17.

In Figure 3.3 we focus on this group, not least because they continue to be followed for one further year (1999–2000). We can see how the proportion of those who have never used a drug reduces with age as more young people try a drug for the first time. Using our four definitions they remain triers/experimenters, if they do not repeat the behaviour and/or indicate that they do not intend to do so in the future. Potential users, on the other hand, expect to take a drug again. They are a growing group in mid adolescence and it is from this transitional status that we would expect to see some migration to the regular drug use status. Importantly, the regular user group is only a small proportion of the overall population.

Although this sector will grow in late adolescence, reaching perhaps between 20 and 25 per cent, we are still only talking about a minority of young people who have become regular drug users by the end of their teens. This said, around 40 per cent of the sample are drug 'active' being potential or regular users, mainly of cannabis.

Table 3.8   Thirteen year olds (year 8) in 1996 and 1998: comparative drugs exposure

	1996 cohort[a] n = 1310 (%)	1998 cohort[c] n = 1441 (%)
Weekly drinkers	28.1	24.6
Current smokers	17.6	10.8
Drug offers/availability	43.3	45.5
Ever tried a drug	25.6	24.0
Past year drug taking	19.2	17.1

a – younger cohort; c – additional cohort.

Comparing Age Cohorts

We surveyed a second cohort of 13 year olds in 1998 (see Table 3.1) using the same schools and the same procedures as utilized in 1996 with the earlier 'year 8' age group. This allows us to make comparisons across time which other survey teams have done so effectively (for example Balding, 1999; Goddard and Higgins, 1999). In Table 3.8 we offer a brief summary comparing the alcohol, tobacco and drugs statuses of these two age cohorts when they were both in year 8 as 13 year olds. We can see how the new younger cohort are consistently slightly less likely to be weekly drinkers and current smokers. Moreover, despite street drugs being more accessible to this next cohort, they are slightly less likely to have ever tried or used at least one illicit drug. This reminds us that the drug involvement of age cohorts, even just a few years apart, can go down as well as up.

Unconventional? Risk and Deviance Factor Analysis

In this section we summarise a complex analysis undertaken with these samples of English adolescents, in search of the risk, abnormal and deviance factors which underpin so much North American drugs discourse and research. We explore whether these English adolescents who try, occasionally use or regularly use illicit drugs are personally, educationally or socially atypical.

Using complete data for 2293 of the respondents, involved in the first two surveys, we undertook both bivariate and multivariate analyses, looking at no less than 42 dependent variables covering all the usually assessed factors, such as ethnicity, family structure, school performance, truancy and so on. It was reassuring in scientific terms that the multivariate analyses were consistent with the bivariate analyses. In short, where we identified statistical significance between our different categories of drugs status (for example triers, regular users) and single factors (for example religion, one parent households), these generally remained significant when we undertook the more sophisticated log linear multivariate analysis, which allows us to assess how different factors inter-play and their relative significance (Aldridge and Parker, 1998). The overall conclusion from these analyses was that there is apparently no clearly defined risk profile which categorically distinguishes those who try drugs from those who don't, or indeed from potential/occasional users and those who abstain. Even in respect of regular use there are few highly statistically significant differences and even where some risk factors were significantly associated with drug use, these did not exclusively or even predominently identify drug involved young people. Until, that is we home in on the 1–2 per cent of the cohort who are involved within a florid drug trying period, which also involves heroin and cocaine (Egginton and Parker, 2000).

Traditionally *gender* predicted drug use whereby we found more young men involved in illegal drug taking. In this study gender was not significant in the younger cohort but being male did slightly predict more regular drug use in the older cohort. Overall, however, gender was not an effective predictor of drugs status at this age. *Religion* was significant only in as much as being a non-believer/atheist predicted more regular drug use when compared with young people who nominate a religious affiliation. *Race* had no great significance nor did the *employment* backgrounds of the young people's parents. We found more statistical significance when we looked at *education* variables. Which school a respondent attended, particularly with age, did predict different levels of drug use. Also, regular drug users were far more likely to dislike school compared with abstainers, who were more likely to enjoy or like school. *Breaking school rules* and truanting was more likely to be the behaviour of drug users than abstainers. However, *school attainment* based on key GCSE results did not predict drug involvement. Academic self assessment was predictive however with those seeing their work as less successful than the year norm more likely to be drug users.

Drug users were more likely to live in *single parent families* and abstainers in two parent families. Drug users tended to have poorer personal relationships with both parents than abstainers. Most importantly *being out in the evenings unsupervised* clearly distinguishes drug triers from abstainers.

Early risk taking was a key predictor of drug use with early smoking and early regular drinking being highly significant indicators of drug trying and use. *Cautions and criminal convictions*, although nearly all for minor offences, were similarly significant.

So are today's young drug takers as 'normal' as their overall age group? Can we identify factors in their background and current life stage which distinguishes them as atypical, unconventional or deviant? The overall answer from this study is – not very clearly and not very well. Differences, even between abstainers and regular drug users, were not so great as to indicate the users were outside 'normal' or normative distributions.

This complexity and lack of major difference between abstainers and users is hardly surprising given the rates of drug trying and use in these samples. If non triers are actually a minority by 16, then we cannot really expect to find definitive personal and social 'abnormalities' in the majority. This said, while the profile of the regular adolescent recreational drug user cannot, factor by factor, generate much statistical significance, what does stand out in the end, as practically significant, is the overall 'package'. In other words we can profile the sort of person who is not only more likely to be a recreational drug user but also, with just a gentle 'push' to the edges of the norm, might also become a problem drug user (see Chapter 6).

The early smoker, early regular drinker (see also Goddard and Higgins, 1999), who is fairly critical of rules and regulations, who is sceptical of school regimes and who likes being out and about socialising from early adolescence and perhaps resents parental supervision and accountability, is far more likely to be both a recreational drug user and, if we add other adverse characteristics and factors, a more problematic user.

However, from this multi-factorial profile we can have diverse outcomes. Young people with these profiles are often also more curious and sceptical. They usually actively generate more disposable income from part-time work to fund going out. These very same characteristics can be found in the significant minority of college/university students who are heavy drinkers and drug users, but eventually become successful high flyers or professionals (for example Makhoul *et al.*, 1998; Webb *et al.*, 1996). In terms of their predecessors, their parents or grandparents during adolescence, today's drug using youth may be unconventional. In terms of their own age cohort, as 1990s youth, they are not.

Conclusion

This study cannot claim to be nationally representative but, on the other hand, it is the only on-going large sample, longitudinal study of adolescent drug trying and use in the UK. The thousands of young people in this study attend largely successful state comprehensive, 'high' and grammar schools and live in typical towns in northern England. The study's main value is in helping us understand the dynamics and complexity of drugs pathways through adolescence and how prevalence data can be generated and interpreted.

The drug trying rates are at the higher end of the 50–70 per cent prevalence rates discovered across the UK, in regional and national youth surveys, but this is because we used particularly sensitive 'disclosure' techniques, followed up non-attenders and with repeat contact built up a degree of trust with the respondents. Furthermore we tend to get higher rates in the north of Britain with whatever method (Miller and Plant, 1996).

We have shown how a more sophisticated approach to measuring drug use statuses can be developed whereby we can distinguish between abstainers, triers, potential users and regular users. Once we do this we find that about 40 per cent of a youth population are 'drug active' but less than half of these are regular users. It seems likely, however, that with age the incremental increase in the proportion of regular drug users will be generated by migration from the potential users – those who have already tried a drug and think they will do so again in the future.

Turning to drugs choices we find that 80 per cent of regular drug use is defined by cannabis. However, both a minority of regular users, potential users and triers have also taken other drugs, notably, nitrites (22 per cent of the older cohort), amphetamines (20 per cent of the older cohort), LSD (13 per cent of the older cohort) and ecstasy (11 per cent of the older cohort). These 'dance drugs' are, as we shall see in Chapters 4 and 5, also related to the 'going out – time out' weekending which leads to the nightclub/dance club scene. The use of these drugs by a small minority of British post-adolescents often begins before access to the nightclub can be fully claimed. However, we can be fairly confident that these early dance drug triers and users will frequently become devotees of, as they see it, brilliant stimulant weekends, which will eventually see cocaine increasingly added to their repertoires.

We also have, in both cohorts, a very small minority of heroin triers and users although we have some doubts about the reliability of some of their returns when we compare annual returns. When we profile them we do tend to find the 'abnormal' characteristics – such as poor parental relationships, lack of supervision, high rates of truancy and petty delinquency, and which do appear to be directly related to their drugs pathways (see Chapter 6). But it is only at the margins that this risk–vulnerability–abnormality search is effective and drug use, often problematic, becomes a further 'symptom' (Sloboda, 1999). The majority of the drug active adolescents in this study are within normative dimensions.

Where abstainers are more home and family centred, drug takers like being out and about with friends. Where abstainers tend to be non-smokers and occasional drinkers, their drug experienced peers nearly all like to drink and most to smoke. The drug involved minority tend to be more critical of rules which constrain their personal preferences and lifestyle and, being out and about, are probably more likely to get into occasional rule breaking scrapes. In the end there are too many people with these characteristics and approaches to life to pathologise, not least because nearly as many are female as male, and such profiles are particularly found in adolescents from professional backgrounds who will in turn go to university and become overtly productive citizens. This reality is not fully faced in official thinking.

This largely conventional identity is also at the heart of the normalisation thesis in respect of adolescent recreational drug use. That conventional, 'ordinary' young people have such easy access to street drugs, that well over half have tried a drug and some four in ten are variously drug involved, is consistent with normalisation. Most importantly, as we shall see in Chapter 4, the way that both abstainers and drug takers become drugwise and coexist is similarly persuasive.

However as we noted in the first chapter, the concept of normalisation is also effective in coping with contraindicators. Normalisation is a two way street. We purposefully compared the drugs status of the 'c' new younger cohort, as 13 year olds, with that of the 'a' younger cohort when they were 13. The key point is that the new 13 year olds in 1998, despite having more access to drugs, had consistently slightly lower rates of drug trying and recent drug taking than their predecessors. They were also less likely to be current smokers and drinkers.

In short, this is a concrete example of how drugs profiles can change through time. Although empirically there are, as yet, only slight grounds (for example Balding, 1999) for believing that the rates of drug involvement may be lower in early adolescents at the new millennium, the key point is that this is always a possibility. Moreover, in our view, if such epidemiological changes do set in they will be largely independent of official interventions as we will demonstrate in Chapter 4.

4
Unpreventable? How Young People Make and Remake Drug Taking Decisions

Jon Breeze, Judith Aldridge and Howard Parker

Purpose

We have argued that significantly reducing the availability of illegal drugs to the youth population is an unachievable short-term goal. We have shown how drug trying and drug use increase across adolescence and illustrated how currently over half of British adolescents try illicit drugs and even by 18 up to one in five are recreational drug users, mainly of cannabis.

This drugs reality has been created across the 1990s and has, unfortunately for official anti-drugs strategists, developed in parallel with an increasingly elaborate delivery of drugs prevention programmes in UK secondary schools. Thus more prevention has coincided with earlier onset, more drug trying and more use. Unmoved by this the national strategy has reinvested in primary prevention across the new decade.

The problem for drugs prevention in the UK is not with the roughly half of the youth population who will remain abstentious by choice but the other half who variously try and use drugs across their adolescence and perhaps into young adulthood.

Given the sheer size of this drug active population and the continuing faith and investment in primary prevention, the absence of a national secondary prevention programme seems like a case of neglect. Once again the explanation for all this is found in the legacy of the war on drugs discourse. It will be several years before the public health imperative is restored and secondary prevention/harm reduction programmes rolled out. The national strategy's goals of reducing Class A drug use (ecstasy, cocaine and heroin) will eventually demand secondary programmes, as

51

will the media's interest in an increasing casualty rate around heroin, cocaine and crack cocaine.

These initiatives will have far more chance of success if they are consistent with and build upon the 'natural' ways young people develop their drugs wisdom. This is why understanding the complexities and dynamism of young people's drugs decision making is so important.

Introduction: Drugwise Youth

How drugwise?

Because, today, street drugs are readily available, talked about and used, then young people, whether or not they take drugs still become relatively *drugwise*. This chapter explores how this drugs wisdom is accumulated and revised continuously right across the teenage years, by describing the journeys individual young people make. This qualitative analysis is based on three consecutive annual interviews (70 completed in all) with a small sample of young people from when they were age 15. This interview group were part of the 'older cohort' found in the longitudinal surveys described in Chapter 3. We are thus also able to see how, at an individual and peer network level, the attitudinal and behavioural population trends described in the longitudinal quantitative analysis, and which are consistent with the national drug use trends described in Chapter 1, are typically generated.

Some drug wisdom is gleaned from talks/conversations (and even confrontations) with parents and from formal drugs education and public health messages but more is generated from informal sources such as television and magazines and, most of all, from everyday observation, conversation and the swapping of 'drugs stories' with other young people. It is also necessary to acknowledge the conclusion from much 1990s research that while young people who do not try illicit drugs (abstainers) rate positively and agree with formal 'say no' drugs education messages, those who are far more sceptical and critical of formal educational inputs are by definition drug triers and drug users. If we are to address this drugs reality then we must also begin to communicate more effectively with young recreational drug triers and users and invest far more in secondary prevention initiatives. Yet how do we 'protect' young drug triers and users from mishap and from becoming problem drug users if the main official vehicles of information/advice/education are 'unconvincing' in the eyes of the very sector (perhaps 30 per cent of young people by 18) 'at risk'? How, for instance, do we attempt to upgrade and sophisticate their very limited knowledge about the dangers of heroin trying and use or 'switching' to cocaine powder because ecstasy has been successfully demonised – if those most 'at risk' are, ironically, the least likely to give credibility to official messengers? If we are to find answers to this drugs prevention dilemma we must first understand how drugs wisdom is generated and updated – how young people make and remake drugs decisions through time. We can then assess how *drugwise* they really are.

Qualitative studies of drugs decision making

We are beginning to understand these decision making processes. A series of qualitative studies of young people's drugs decision making has developed in recent years. These local studies appear to have been carried out wholly independently of each other and yet all but one reach remarkably similar conclusions. Five studies (but see also Bell *et al.*, 1998; Coffield and Gofton, 1994) have described, although using different terms, a cost–benefit 'consumerist' framework, which becomes apparent when we listen to and reflect upon young people's accounts. This decision making involves assessing the risk of taking each distinctive street drug and developing management strategies which involve either keeping away from a particular substance altogether (Young and Jones, 1997) or learning to use the drug in 'sensible' ways (Boys *et al.*, 1998; Hart and Hunt, 1997; Hirst and McCamley-Finney, 1994). Each young person informally draws up a hierarchy of safety–danger for the most widely available drugs (for example solvent/gases, 'poppers', cannabis, amphetamines, LSD, ecstasy). Consensus is greatest around cannabis at the least dangerous end of the spectrum and heroin and crack cocaine at the other, although ecstasy is seen as far more dangerous by today's under 16 year olds than those who grew up in the early 1990s. Views on amphetamines, tranquillisers and LSD are far more diverse. Risk assessment revolves around immediate health risks, being ill, having bad trips, insomnia but also 'getting caught' or being dependent on drugs. The benefits and gains are distinctive to each drug ranging from being mellow and relaxed, to acquiring self confidence and sociability, to sustained energy, to simply 'buzzing' or 'getting wrecked' and, in social terms, having fun with friends.

These studies also emphasize that most young people's drug use is recreational and thus another skill is to fit these drug taking episodes into one's everyday conventional life priorities – studying, working, maintaining romantic relationships and one's social circle (Boys *et al.*, 1998; Perri 6, 1997). In short, a strong rational purposeful strand of decision making is at work, whereby, certain types of recreational drug use are seen to enhance leisure time (Boys *et al.*, 1998; Young and Jones, 1997).

All these studies found that most young people, and indeed most young drug users in the *mid* 1990s, continued to recognize the dangers of heroin and crack cocaine use, vowing never to try these drugs. However, significantly, two of the studies specifically conclude that because drugs wisdom relies so heavily on informal peer related knowledge it may be incomplete or inaccurate (Hart and Hunt, 1997; Young and Jones, 1997). Unfortunately because all these investigations were reported as one-off snapshot studies we have no sense of how drugs wisdom develops with age and life experience or mutates through time or adapts to the now ready availability of particular drugs whether potentially benign (herbal highs) or clearly dangerous (heroin, GHB).

Both this study (for example, Measham *et al.*, 1998) and the only other longitudinal investigation into adolescent drugs decision making conducted during the 1990s (Parker *et al.*, 1998) are able to extend and hopefully sophisticate our knowledge about young people's drugs journeys right through adolescence. The NW Longitudinal Study was for instance able to show how local youth populations will contain a significant minority of abstainers who maintain their status and a consistent anti-drugs perspective right across adolescence although this usually modifies with age to accommodate the behaviour of 'sensible' drug taking peers. The majority, however, whether drug experimenters or drugs users, while they have their own individualised rules and boundaries, hold more pro recreational drug use attitudes which are consistent with their actual behaviour. They feel comfortable with their drug use and while apprehensive about adult reactions certainly felt no significant guilt (Parker *et al.*, 1998).

The one small study in conflict with the conclusion that this cost–benefit consumerist perspective to 'recreational' drug use is internally consistent and widely utilized in young people's drugs decision making (that is Shiner and Newburn, 1996) was based on interviews with a group of primarily early adolescents, three quarters of whom had *never* tried a drug and who had just attended anti-drugs workshops at which the researchers had actually been present. In these circumstances we should not be surprised that the authors found most interviewees offered them an anti-drugs perspective. This report concluded that young people feel guilty about drug taking but neutralise this guilt by blaming peer pressure for leading them into drug use (Shiner and Newburn, 1996), a conclusion in line with official drugs prevention discourses emphasizing 'resistance' and 'risk' but not reached by any of the other recent qualitative studies.

The Qualitative Methods

In-depth interviews were undertaken with a small sample of 27, then pupils of three schools in two different regions of northern England. They were first interviewed in 1996 when they were year 10 15 year olds. The interviews were voluntary, they were arranged discretely and initially undertaken in a private room in each school. Each interviewee received a £10 music token for their time. Interviews lasted around 45 minutes on average, slightly less with 'abstainers' and often over an hour with drug triers and users. One young male interviewer (Jon Breeze) undertook almost all the interviews right across the series, thereby facilitating a sense of trust. All interviews were tape recorded and comprehensively transcribed. They were also cross-checked with the annual survey questionnaire returns for each interviewee.

The second leg of the interviews suffered from some attrition, whereby after letters and telephone calls only 21 of the original cohort were reinterviewed in the summer of 1997. However three more young people from the survey cohort were 'added' and interviewed, giving a total of 24. The third leg involved successfully reinterviewing 19 of the 24. Of these seventeen were interviewed for the third time and two for the second time. Table 4.1 describes the regional location, educational/occupational status and gender of the subjects.

The key difference in the third and final round of interviews was the location. Fifteen of the sample were interviewed in their own homes and the remaining four in other neutral venues (for example, leisure centre, friend's house). This relocation arose from the fact that half the respondents had left school but was also a consequence of everyone voluntarily giving SPARC home telephone numbers and addresses in 1997. When recontacted, therefore, this gave each young person options – including inviting the interviewer to their home. Our respondents clearly took steps to ensure complete privacy was created. Most often their parents or other family members were out or 'sent' by the interviewees to other parts of the house or into the garden. In one meeting the interviewer asked if he could check a parent was out of earshot. Interviewees were asked about the new interview venue. While most had found a private room in school satisfactory in previous years they nearly all commented that the home venue was even better. They felt relaxed and in control of the situation and able to be wholly assertive with any family members requiring 'relocation'.

Table 4.1 Interview cohort: summary of drugs status at 14–17 years

ID (n = 19)	In education or work	Sex	→ 1	→ 2	→ 3 (years)
292050	E	F	Drug user cannabis, multiple trier	Heroin trier Heroin user	→ Poly drug 'problem' user
292039	W	M	Abstainer	Abstainer	→ Cannabis trier
292101	W	F	Cannabis user	Occasional cannabis user	→ Cannabis only user
292092	W	M	Abstainer	Abstainer	→ Abstainer
282146	E	M	Abstainer	Abstainer Popper trier	→ Basic Abstainer
282052	E	F	Abstainer	Abstainer	→ Amphetamine trying
282167	W	F	Abstainer	Cannabis trier	→ LSD trier
282057	W	M	Abstainer	Abstainer	→ Abstainer
282066	W	M	Cannabis trier	Occasional cannabis user	→ Cannabis user, LSD, amphetamine trier
142010	E	F	Abstainer	Abstainer	→ Abstainer
142043	W	F	Cannabis trier	Occasional cannabis user	→ Poppers → LSD trier
142004	E	F	Cannabis, LSD, poppers, amphetamine	continued	→ continued recreational drug user
142038	E	F	Abstainer	Abstainer	→ Abstainer
142022	E	M	Cannabis user	Reduced to occasional user	→ Non user, in-transition
142185	E	M	Cannabis user → multiple trier	LSD, tranquillisers	→ Drug user
142023	W	M	Abstainer	Abstainer	→ Abstainer
142160	E	F	Abstainer	Abstainer	→ Abstainer
142163	W	M	Abstainer	Abstainer	→ Cannabis trying
142008	E	F	Abstainer	Cannabis trier	→ Former trier

New Social Rites

Early risk takers who begin smoking, drinking and trying drugs such as cannabis from around age 12 onwards tend to be found in peer groups with some 'older' members who have access to drugs and know how to take them. These social groupings tend to meet initially in semi-public places (for example, parks, bus shelters) or seek out a private room in someone's house. These drug taking opportunities increase across adolescence as 'unsupervised' time increases and rights to privacy, staying out or over and going to 'real' parties increase.

At around age 17 there is an important rite of passage. After final public exams (GCSEs) you can leave school. From here moving to the Sixth Form or Further Education or getting a job, starting a modern apprenticeship, signing on for a New Deal or perhaps just disappearing into the shadows to make ends meet in other ways – are the main options. Each of our young subjects has been involved in one or more of these changes. One consequence of these processes is to facilitate the development of additional or alternative friendship networks:

> I get quite a lot of money now, and I've got another mate who works as well, it's just like exploded, getting loads of new clothes and stuff like that. My other mates who are like at school, they can't afford to go out, or they're doing these training schemes where they get like forty-five pounds a week. . . . It's like working now, I don't get to see my mates that much during the week, so at weekends when we're going out we go into town. So it's pretty much 'going out', more than just going up to their houses and stuff like that.
>
> [*So are you drinking more now?*]
>
> I am actually. Because I've started working, my dad had sort of . . . I've been paying board, so he's been like bringing a few four packs home for me. Also its like – 'Oh I can't be bothered cooking tonight, come on we'll go up to the pub'. We'd be going out twice a week, having some alcohol in the house, and then going out Friday night and going out Saturday night. (292039 male, 17 yrs)

Even for those still living at home but only just getting by doing part-time casual work locally the tendency to 'go out' has also increased:

> Spending time with my mates. They're mates that I've been with all my life. We're in the pub a lot, like through the week and at weekends if we've got some money we'll try to make a night of it. Just to

enjoy ourselves basically. When I was about fourteen there wasn't really much to do, but now I've grown up I can go into pubs and what have you.... I used to go out last year, but now I look a bit older so I go out a bit more. I just go out all the time. I didn't actually do that last year, I used to play a lot of sports, I've stopped... well I still play football once a week, but not as much as I used to. (282066 male, 17 yrs)

This emphasis on going out, travelling further afield to new venues and for new experiences is shared by most interviewees quite independently of their drugs status, as these drug abstainers illustrate:

It's at Wigan. A few of my mates, and me and my sister, and some of her mates are going down in cars. It'll be alright. We went to see Oasis in Manchester, at the G-Mex, they were brilliant. I'm off to Robbie Williams as well, at Manchester Apollo. (292039 male, 17 yrs)

On Saturday I went out, going to pubs and that around Huddersfield and we ended up in a club, so it was alright.
[*What are the most important things about your spare time?*]
I don't know, socialising I suppose.... Now that I've got a job I feel as though I've made something.... I've done that... when you interviewed me before I said I was looking forward to getting some work done. Now I'm alright I can get on with my life and work my way up.... I see a lot more of them (work mates) now. I hardly see my mates from school and my other mate, we go out sometimes but not as much as we did. My work mates are who I hang around with most. (292092 male, 17 yrs)

However, the pinnacle of this socialising is found on Friday and Saturday nights, visiting the local regional centres with their conspicuous night life. Here too the previously cautious and conservative find new leisure activities and often join the dominant mode – circuit drinking till closing time then on to the nightclub:

I listen to a lot more dance music since I started going out a lot more... we go down to the town and drink in pubs and stuff. We start in the Bull, we work our way down, we've got a route set out that we always go on. We go to the Mad House because the drinks are cheap even though its a bit crappy. Then we go down to Jammers because my friend loves the music there. Then we sometimes go to the Volts if we've got time but we haven't actually been there for ages. Then we usually go into Shrimps because everybody meets at nine o'clock ... then we go to the Coffee Shop because we like to get a Pink Kangaroo. I love them. . . . By the end of the night we're usually so drunk that we say we'll go anywhere. Then we usually split off and go different ways.

[*How many of you usually go out?*]

It's like a huge reunion, everybody sees each other. Then we usually meet up with all the lads out of our year and the year above in the town.

[*Are you going out more this year than last?*]

Yeah definitely. We've started hanging around with the lads out of the Upper Sixth ... and they go to town every single Friday. I'd get bored if I did that. Last year we'd just go say if it was the end of term or something but now we go a couple of times a month, we go out quite a lot now. (142160 female, Northumbria)

In terms of drugs decisions a number of significant implications begin to emerge as a consequence of this new emphasis on going out and 'time out'. First, it involves many young people in drinking far more alcohol, a potent drug in itself. This in turn acts as both a way of experiencing and 'dealing with' intoxication through social support but also through 'disinhibition' plays its role in creating a situation where decision making becomes less well planned and sometimes, in retrospect, ill conceived. Second, simply being out and about in the pub–bar–club setting exposes young people, whatever their drug status, to far more availability of a wider range of street drugs. The cannabis smoking seen in the local pub becomes cannabis, amphetamine, ecstasy and cocaine powder being given, shared or sold in the busy nightlife of town or city centre. Third, the scale of drugs use is far greater as 'weekend' users congregate and because all this is experienced in extended friendship – acquaintance networks then 'support' for new drugs experiences is accentuated.

As we shall see nearly all the decisions to take the first or another drug at this life stage can be located or traced to this 'enhanced' social context.

Abstainers' Journeys

Steadfast abstainers

These year on year interviews have provided an ideal opportunity to trace and define how 'abstainers' maintain or modify their attitudes and behaviour across adolescence. Clearly the surveys have shown this population group shrinking in size whereby those who have never tried a drug become a minority by the end of adolescence. This said, if we sum abstainers with those who only try a drug in adolescence or, although they try or use for a while actually give up any further illicit drug use – then the majority are in practical terms still abstainers.

These interviews reinforce the findings of most other studies – that many abstainers come to accommodate the drugs talk and use of their peers. Abstainers become *drugwise* in their own terms because most have to negotiate in everyday worlds where drugs are routinely available and talked about. Some will remain totally against any illegal drug taking, however, and as steadfast abstainers continue to have absolutely no truck with drug trying or drug use. Three of these 'classic' abstainers were in the interview sample. For them drug use is wrong – morally, legally and pragmatically. Their interviews tend to be briefer since they annually, honestly restate their attitudinal and 'ideological' position and offer little elaboration. Moreover because they are more home and family centred and have not joined their peers on the town, pubbing and clubbing, they have less contact with drug talk, drug offers and drug use. This type of abstentious young person is highly unlikely to become involved in risk taking leisure.

[*Take your time and have a look through this list. Have you ever had any of the drugs in the list?*]
   No.
   [*... since we last met ... have you been around when any of these drugs were available or offered, either free or for money, so you probably could have had them if you want to?*]
   No.
   [*None of them?*]
   No.
   [*Do you think any of your friends ever use drugs?*]
   Not that I know of.
   [*Do you ever talk to your friends about drugs?*]
   Not really.
   [*Take your time and have another look through the list for me. Are there any drugs ... you think you may try at some point in the future?*]
   No.
   [*Can you tell me a bit about anything that might change your mind?*]

I don't think I would change my mind because I don't take them. (142038 female, abstainer, 17 yrs)

Two other interviewees offered almost identical sets of responses to these questions emphasizing that they rarely if ever found themselves in situations where drugs were available, or socialised with other people who tried or used drugs. They also believed that their neighbourhood 'is not really the sort of area where they [drug users] are' (142008 female). 'I don't think I avoid it, I just think it doesn't happen.' (142010 female)

Drugwise abstainers

Other respondents who had continued to either reject drug trying or been in only the most benign trying episodes (whereby they have done no more than sniff poppers or take one pull on a cannabis joint), continue to become more *drugwise*.

This is directly related to their outgoing sociability and keenness to join the 'time out' activities of pubbing and clubbing but as drugfree participants:

> [*Are you going to pubs or anything like that?*]
> Yeah, quite often really, when I've got the money to. I always go down even if its just for a pint and a game of pool, even though I'm underage. . . . I've never been turned away from one yet.
> [*Are you going to the pub more often than you were last year?*]
> Definitely yeah . . . well over Christmas it was nearly every other day. Now I'm struggling for money, I'm saving for a holiday, so now its more like two or three times a week.

This young man had been around all the street drugs except legal herbal drugs and heroin. He had been in situations where friends had tried LSD and acquaintances had 'rolled up' and smoked cannabis in local pubs.

> Nobody was really bothered, they just took it out and did it in public, it was no big deal.

On clubbing nights ecstasy had been offered:

> . . . this really big fellow came up to me and slapped me on the back, he said 'Are you alright lads, are you having a good time?' I said 'Yeah'. He said 'Do you want to buy some Es?' I said I had already got

some, so he left me alone. My friend who lives in the pub . . . he's gone to get them before and he's showed me little bags of them, little snap bags.

His most recent unwanted experience was being in a locked classroom with a fellow pupil who was weighing out cocaine to sell in nightclubs in Leeds. He felt real discomfort to be involved in probably the most 'coercive' situation reported during this study:

I was a bit nervous because I was thinking if any of the teachers came, I know I would be booted out straight away even though it was nothing to do with me. I was really nervous.

Summing up he felt

. . . just different times when I've been around different people and they've shown me little bags of stuff or whatever they've got. It's too numerous to remember really. It seems to have got worse this past year. I've been around it more and more. I'm sort of very passive about it, when I've been offered drugs I just think it's another knob-head. (282146 male, abstainer, 17 yrs)

Several other non triers had found themselves in drug offer situations far more often over the past year.

When I went in there (local pub) there was this other guy there and he was rolling up. He said 'Do you want some?' I said 'No because I'm just off to work', I didn't want to do it anyway . . . I might do it if you were allowed to do it but seeing as its illegal NO. (282057 male, abstainer, 17 yrs)

Getting used to these situations is a necessary concession for those non drug users who like going out drinking and socialising in large groups:

If I saw some I wouldn't gasp like I would before, because you see people all the time now who you know have been on them and you know have got them. My mates still take it (cannabis/speed) and I don't know what they'll go onto next. They say you start on cannabis and you go onto something bigger. I don't think they will but I don't know. (292092 male, abstainer, 17 yrs)

Drug Triers

Situational triers

There are clearly, in any representative UK youth population, a significant minority who have already and might in the future, occasionally try an illegal substance. Many see this event as benign and fairly insignificant. Yet for some such episodes reinforce their general view that they can have a good time or manage the bad without any chemical assistance. They suffer little cognitive dissonance because they hold fairly neutral attitudes to drugs and their use by others and because they feel comfortable with drug users and confident in their own ability to make appropriate drugs decisions. One drug trier, really an occasional user, who will smoke cannabis if it is offered in certain social settings but will go many months without doing so again, previously reported no strong desire to try other drugs. However at age 17 he felt his attitudes and intentions might be changing and that he might now try other drugs.

> Probably, yeah. I think its softened towards it. . . . I think its because it was around me, just like friends doing it. (142163 male, trier, Northumbria)

This situational or setting related drug trying affected another young man who spent most of his social time going out getting drunk with friends:

> When you go out, you might get a bit drunk, well I've had a few blasts on that cannabis, but that's only been about once or twice when I've not been in a sane head. But none of the others [drugs].

This cannabis trier did not particularly enjoy his smoking experience and saw no point 'learning' to enjoy it through practice because he saw that as commensurate with *deciding* to be a smoker and cannabis user. He felt that curiosity, the social setting and his drinking produced the situation for 'having a blast on someone's joint'.

> It was like – go on then I'll have a try. A lot of people do it so there's got to be something to it. So you just try it.
> [*So if you didn't enjoy the experience why do you try it again?*]
> That's the question isn't it. Really again, you just get with a group of people. . . . There's been no sustained use, you just have a pull on it and that was it – 'that's not nice'. I suppose that's as good an education

for somebody who's never ever tried it before, just like to try it once, because you're not going to like it. With cannabis you can do that and not get any consequences. If you tried with something like E, well it's different isn't it.

[*How do you mean different?*]

If you try E once, that's it, that could kill you. Like that Leah Betts kid, she just did one. So it's different, you know there is a minimal risk. There's practically no risk whatsoever if you just have one pull on a joint.

[*Do you think you'll try cannabis again?*]

I'd like to think no, but you don't know do you. I wouldn't have said that I would have tried it once, it was just a decision that arose and you have to make spot decisions.

[*In what sort of situation do you think you might try it again?*]

I'd like to think that I wouldn't, but if you're with a group of your mates and they're all doing it. . . . There's a few of my mates who do smoke it quite heavily. There's me and this other lad, Paul, he doesn't either, but all our mates around us, so its like – 'oh go on then, I'll just have a little dabble'. (292039 male, drug trier, 17 yrs)

These occasional 'situational' drug users, although they seem almost reluctant initiates, do acknowledge that they may repeat their behaviour whereas other triers vow they will not.

Former trier–users

In keeping with the dynamism and change in drugs statuses documented throughout this study we have again found respondents who have, at least temporarily, given up drug trying or occasional use. One young woman who had taken LSD and cannabis several times since last interviewed had also not done so in recent months and classified herself as a former user. She now articulated fairly negative views about drug use focusing on their potential dangers. She based this on direct contact with users and drug stories about local events. She fully accepted her earlier drug taking was made of personal choice, rejecting any suggestion of peer pressure:

No it was just because I felt like it and I wanted to. It was all down to me.

And while her experiences had been benign and enjoyable she noted that others she knew had been less fortunate:

Well my boyfriend got poorly off Es and I've seen my cousin and she's addicted to speed and she's on it all the time and my friend died of methadone and heroin and she went to my school.

All this has convinced her not to try drugs again in the future:

[*Have your opinions or attitudes towards drugs changed over the last year?*]
Yeah. Well I know definitely not to do them because of my friend dying and what happened to my boyfriend and the way my cousin's been. So I know I'll keep away. (282167 female, former user, 17 yrs)

Another young woman from the same town reached similar conclusions partly because of a change in friendship groups including a 'new' boyfriend:

He used to smoke it, he used to smoke cigarettes, and the last time he smoked cannabis was the last time I smoked it. I don't even like it being smoked around me because...like and he's got asthma anyway so won't smoke it.
[*That's the only drug he's ever had?*]
Yeah, he feels the same as me. We know some people who have taken ecstasy and things, and we've both said it's stupid so I know he won't take anything like that.

Moreover, becoming a drug user requires the initiate to enjoy or learn to enjoy or value the experience. This was simply not happening for this respondent:

[*Can you tell me a bit about the last time you had it?*]
I don't know why I do it actually, because like...smoking, I used to smoke when I was at school, for about three weeks, and it didn't do anything for me, so...and when I drink, that doesn't do anything either, unless I drink loads. When I smoked some cannabis it didn't do anything for me either, so I suppose I was doing it and it wasn't doing anything to me, so I was thinking there was no harm in it. But then...I've got like really small lungs, so if somebody offered me some I'd just say no. It didn't do anything for me anyway, so I thought what's the point.
[*So when was the last time?*]
About autumn. We were down Kirkby outside, with our friends from Kirkby.

[*How many times have you had it since I last interviewed you?*]
About three times.
[*How did you smoke it?*]
Just a spliff.
[*Did you ever buy it?*]
No I'd never buy it.
[*Do you think you'll ever have cannabis again?*]
No, because it doesn't do anything for me. There's like no point. Some people do it because it calms them down, but it doesn't calm me down. Some people do it because they think they get a buzz from it, it doesn't do that for me. So it's like I'm taking something, and all it's doing is making me rubbish, so I won't have it again. (292101 female, former trier, 17 yrs)

'Giving up' is sometimes a consequence of the propensity to transfer between the illicit and licit which has occurred in many of the drugs careers monitored. One young male having been a fairly regular cannabis smoker in the past felt that over the last year he'd pretty well given up smoking, having found the new 'rite' of going out drinking with friends a far more enjoyable way of spending both time and money:

I just went off it. I just didn't see the appeal of it anymore. I saw my mates wasting their time on it, and I got a bit more into drinking, going to town spending all my money ... well not all my money, I'm not an alcoholic or anything. I've just been spending more money on beer and going out. I just thought that's a lot better, just appreciate a good ale as opposed ...
[*So why do you think it's better?*]
It's a good question that. I don't know, it's just a lot more social. I mean you're sitting and you're smoking cannabis and you're like sitting depressed or your sitting and you're not very energetic. I like to be the opposite, go to the town and have a good laugh and you're talking to a lot of people, it's social, it's good.
[*Do you think you'll ever have it again?*]
Probably, aye.
[*Why do you think you'll have it again?*]
I'm not like really, determined. ... I'm not like anti-cannabis or anything. I've still got mates who do it now and again. I've got two mates who are like regular every night smokers. I'm not really anti it, I'm just sort of like not really bothered about it.

Asked if he might try any others drugs in the future:

> Possibly LSD because I've never had it. I think curiosity might have its wicked way. I'd probably have that one, but I'm not going to intently set out to take it or nothing though. Maybe ecstasy. You get all these tales – 'Oh it's the best thing I've ever had'. I might have one out of curiosity I suppose.
>
> [*So if you wouldn't mind trying them in the future, why haven't you tried them so far?*]
>
> I don't know. The likes of ecstasy, I've never really been exposed to it. I go to town now and again, but I don't really go clubbing much, well I've only been clubbing once. I don't really go out with those sorts of people. There's the odd person who has a smoke of cannabis, but... that's as far as it goes.
>
> [*What are the effects of LSD that make you think you wouldn't mind trying it?*]
>
> I don't know, it's just I've heard people talking about all the trips they've had with little purple people hitting them in the ankles with bats and stuff. It's just like it's wacky, and I'm curious.
>
> [*What are the effects of ecstasy that you wouldn't mind experiencing?*]
>
> Don't know, it's just people say it's a good rush and it's the best time of your life, I just want to see why. (142022 male, 17 yrs)

In terms of pathways or drugs journeys this young man is *a potential user* as defined in the last chapter (see also Parker *et al.*, 1998). He may well continue not to take any illicit drugs in the immediate future but because he is drug experienced, has had no dire consequences and is contemplating trying other drugs he is likely to do so in the future. It is this complexity which requires us, conceptually at least, to link a particular drugs status at any one time with the likely future behaviour of each individual.

Starters at seventeen

One interviewee had talked assertively about her commitment to abstinence. At age 15 she was angry with girl friends and her new boyfriend for taking drugs. At age 16 she felt embarrassed at her increasing tolerance as a *drugwise* abstainer.

> I thought 'oh god what am I going to say 'cos everything has changed so much you know. I'm not related to them (the researchers whom she assumes are opposed to drug use) as much as I was back then.

I'm not as shocked by it [drug use] as I was back then. I've just got used to the idea of it all.

At age 17, having split up with the drug using boyfriend, she had begun going out pubbing and clubbing with a group of female friends. This had involved a steep learning curve in relation to drinking, intoxication and indeed being sick from several 'girley nights out':

> I just split up with John and I started going out with Sal and every-one. There was me, Sally and Carla in Sal's room drinking wine. Me and Sal were paralytic, we went into the bathroom thinking we were going to be ill soon. Cath was banging on the door saying the bus is here, the bus stop is just outside the door. We missed the bus. Me and Sal were sat on the door step and Sal was sick. This was the first time I had gone to Halifax with them after I split up with John. I felt a bit better so I walked to the bus stop. I was leaning against the bus stop and I started to feel ill again. Sal decided to rub my back and I was sick again. This was me, respectable Tina being sick at the road side. I was calling them fuckers because they had made me this way. I was going – 'You fuckers, look what you've done to me.' I was being violently ill. Sal was laughing, she was going – 'You'll feel much better, that's it just be sick.' That was the funniest, but you had to be there obviously.

This young woman's drugs initiation is best recounted in full as she perceived it:

> The first week, I'd seen John with another girl, and he was com-pletely flaunting it in front of me, I was just having a bad night. I was really ill, I had too much wine, I was being violently ill in this horrible club. A bouncer came to check on me, to check that I wasn't dead, because I was slumped on the toilet. There was this girl outside going – 'I think she's in trouble, go and get the bouncer.' He was bang-ing on the door and I was just going – 'Go away.' He was saying – 'Stand up.' I just went – 'No.' I could stand up. I just didn't want to. But I stood up and he opened the door, and he said – 'Oh she's fine', so I carried on hurling. The week after that I was really ill again, just from drinking. I hadn't drank a lot, it was just I was drinking wine, because I don't like lager and I couldn't afford spirits. I was ill off that. So I thought I'll have cider this week. We were watching my friend in the band in Bradford. Then we went back to my friends

Mandy's and we had a few drinks there, and then we went into town. It didn't even cross my mind to do it, but I was having a really good night, and I thought right ... I started feeling a tiny bit sick as well, even though I hadn't had a lot to drink. Sal ran into the toilets and went – 'Tina, Tina come here.' I went in and she started taking this speed, she said – 'Do you want some? I promise you I won't give you enough to make you ill.' She said – 'I'll give you a tiny bit.' So I thought – 'I'm not going to have a bad night again this week.' So I took it. It was merely out of curiosity as well, just to see what it would do. Took it and it didn't do a thing, it made me more awake, that's all it did. I think it hit me Sunday morning, when all my relatives came around. I was actually talking to them, which I usually don't, but was actually quite chatty. Anyway, I took the speed, I was a bit more awake, everything was really good, a really good night. On the night rider home, I made the bus driver stop outside my house so I didn't have to walk anywhere. I came in, I was awake all night, I was freezing cold. I went hot, cold, hot, cold, on my own, awake, thinking – 'I don't like this, I really don't like this.' I woke up in the morning and I had to face all my relatives and my dad, he came over just to see me. He noticed my hands were really cold, and looked into my eyes, and I was obviously a bit alert. He asked me if I was all right, and that really did panic me. I said – 'Oh I'm fine.' I think I got a delayed reaction off it, because I wanted to talk to my mum in the morning, just talk about anything, but she wasn't having any of it, she was stressed with organising the buffet. I was dying for her to talk to me and she wouldn't, so I got really upset.

[*So what time did you take it?*]
't must have been at about half eleven.
[*So how long did you stay at the club?*]
Until half past two.
[*So did you not feel anything while you were in the club?*]
Just more awake, it just made me feel more awake, but I didn't feel sick or dizzy or ... I heard people say – you might want to dance, but I didn't. I did but it wasn't the drug that was making me want to dance, I wanted to do it of my own accord. I wasn't having that much of a good time, but then I was, like just talking to people, that's all it made me do.
[*So you were more talkative?*]
Yeah, just more lively I think.
[*Did it make you more energetic?*]
Yeah, definitely.

[*How was it when you were in the club? Was it good or bad?*]

I wasn't panicking at all, because I had all my friends around me and I knew I hadn't done as much as anyone in that club. I knew that there was people who was in there who hadn't done a thing, and knew I had done something, and they would look after me. I had so many friends around me who just weren't going to let anything happen to me. All of them knew what I'd done, they knew how much I'd taken. I never thought I'd try it at all. In my questionnaire I said I might, but I had no idea that I would on Saturday. It just happened.

Given the recency of this initiation and the pace of change in her life this interviewee spoke of her moral dilemmas, her concerns about friends who did too many drugs, her commitment not to take ecstasy and her shame at 'letting down' her close abstaining friend.

I disappointed Cath . . . she was really annoyed with me and her opinion matters so much to me. She was like – 'How could you? I thought you were with me.' I know how it feels to be out with loads of people on drugs and you're not, so it's . . . I don't think I will. I won't do anymore than I did that Saturday night. I'm too scared, I'm too weak, I'm scared I'll die or something. I'll collapse and then just manage to live to get an arsing off my parents the day after. That's just my luck. But I knew that off that much . . . I really didn't feel I was going to be in any danger, because I had so little. But then I don't know that, because I don't know the facts.

This said, asked if she will take amphetamines again:

Speed – probably yeah but no more than I took on Saturday night if I do. (282052 female, drug trier, 17 yrs)

Tina had changed drugs status from abstainer to trier and with the softening of her anti-drug attitudes and her new social environment is in pathways terms also *a potential user*. Spending far more time with an expanded 'fun' peer group, going drinking in town, clubbing and being with others talking about and taking drugs, being disinhibited, feeling 'safe' with *drugwise* friends, taking a small dose of a particular drug she regarded as 'less dangerous' – all these factors emerge from this young woman's account. Despite her apparent 'spontaneity' Tina is one respondent who has given much thought to 'recreational' drug use over the nearly three years she was followed. At age 16 she was perceptively contemplating that a Saturday night out would lead to a drug initiation. Her drugs journey will continue as will her willingness and commitment to assess the 'morality' of her behaviour. Nice girls *do* do drugs.

Becoming Drug Users

Several interviewees had extended their drug trying and drug use experiences over the previous year. One young man who had already become a regular cannabis user spending £25 a week on his 'quarter' and occasionally using LSD and amphetamines, insisted at age 16, that he would never touch ecstasy. Reminded of this he offered the following explanation.

> Yeah, because I used to think ecstasy was a bad thing. When people used to take ecstasy, I used to look at them as a bad person, but it's not a bad drug ecstasy really. People just make it out to be bad, like with Leah Betts dying and what have you. People only die because . . . she took one didn't she, and she died off it, but that was only because she was boozing and dancing at the same time. You can't do that on ecstasy and speed, because your heart skips a beat every time . . . you know when you're dancing and you get really hot, and your heart's beating, it skips a beat, and it doesn't help you at all. If you just take one, or if you just take half at a time, half every two hours, and you just bring yourself up, you'll be all right. When you want to drink, drink water or still orange, don't drink beer. That's why people make them out to be a bad thing, because [of] people dying. They only die because they take five at a time and what have you. Like I say I used to look at people as if it was a bad thing, but it doesn't really bother me now ecstasy at all. Speed – naw, like I say I've had a quarter of a line and I thought – 'fuck that'. I heard that's the biggest drug killer, speed.

This interviewee had also recently come into contact with cocaine powder for the first time at a friend of a friend's house. Having noted its use in the local serious recreational scene he felt cocaine might be worth trying at some point in the future.

> Charlie maybe, cocaine, because its a rich man's drug apparently, so I probably will try that . . . if its that expensive for what it is it must be a good thing. So I'd probably try that but heroin no never.

[*Why do you think that about heroin?*]

Because it's addictive, and you just change when you're on heroin because you go out stealing, and you're a bad person, you spread HIV and shit like that. Fuck that for a game of cricket, its horrible.... You hear about heroin all the time. My brother's mate's mates, they're big smackheads. When I lived in Blackpool, it's full of smackheads, you see them, they're in their own little world, and they're dirty all the time. (282066 male, drug user, 17 yrs)

Another interviewee had also extended her drug trying beyond cannabis. She had rejected an amphetamine trying offer prior to the second year interview because she regarded the drug as having too many dangerous side effects. LSD, she had argued a year ago, was tempting but again too unpredictable. A year on and a *Tellytubbies Tinkywinky* acid blotter later she found the trip:

> ...funny because I didn't feel anything and then I started seeing things and that and I got the giggles. I was alright and I went to lie down in the lad's room. He had like funny wallpaper and I was tripping off the wallpaper.... It was good. I was worried at first because everybody says you get bad trips and all that, I was dead worried. One of the lads said – 'Just don't think about it, just take it and don't think anything about it.' I just blanked my mind and thought of other things, and I was alright.

Convinced she will never take ecstasy or tranquillisers because of what she has seen of young people in her area who have done so this young woman also recognized that at last year's interview she had said the same about LSD.

> I thought I would never ever take LSD or that and that I'd (not) be offered speed as much but I have been. (142043 female, drug user, 17 yrs)

Being part of a social group containing several amphetamine users it seems possible she will complete her experience of the repertoire of 'dance drugs' in due course. This switching or expanding the repertoire of drugs is routinely found in the journey to becoming a drug user (Boys *et al.*, 1998; Measham *et al.*, 2000; Parker *et al.*, 1998).

Emily, a young woman in the midst of trying a range of drugs at age 16, had also continued her drugs journey. A daily cannabis user who enjoys LSD occasionally and amphetamines for nights out she regards ecstasy as a dangerous drug.

> E is just naughty. You hear about people getting bad from it, people dying from it. You don't go out on a night out and say I'm going to have an E and have a really good time tonight, because of all the stuff you hear you can't possibly have a good time because you are forever thinking – what if it happens to me, what if it's me, what if I dehydrate, what if I drink too much water, what if I think I'm a skydiver and jump off the top of a building. It's just not my kind of thing, it's just not what I want.

The contingencies associated with drug using networks can override such apparent caution about taking 'riskier' drugs however.

> I had been out in town, and I had met up with a couple of friends that I hadn't seen for like ages. We went back to his house, and we were all just sitting with joints, buckets, lines of whizz. Passing them around. Somebody went – 'there's a line for you'. I just automatically thought it was whizz. I was like – 'wooo'. They went – 'Ha ha that was coke'. I was like – 'Oh shit'. I went to sleep, and then I woke up and I was like . . . I don't know if it was because I had had whizz and alcohol, and then coke, but I felt really terrible. Cannabis, I use regularly, and whizz, I use that regularly, but I've never felt like that. And you don't want to go out and spend your money on this kind of thing and feel terrible for two days after it, there's just no point.

Emily's boyfriend discourages her drug use while her best female friends are heavy recreational drug users to the point of also doing some dealing. Her best friend was, at the time of interview, remanded in custody for cannabis dealing having got involved with another woman selling drugs. Our respondent, given her reputation as a drug user, is also getting involved in providing drugs for friends. Asked about her cannabis use she remarked:

> It's a social thing, it wouldn't be any fun sitting and having a smoke on your own. You just don't have a session on your own, you've got to have other people with you. My friends from school, they come along and say – 'can you get me a deal?' I'm like – 'all right I'll get you a deal'. I get them a deal and they'll sit here, my room's not very big but sometimes I've got like eight people in there, and my room's

just totally yellow, full of smoke. But we do, we have a really good laugh. But I wouldn't sit on my own, no.

This young woman has thus far selected cannabis, LSD and amphetamines as her drugs of choice. She has a taboo against pills, particularly ecstasy and tranquillisers based on a bad personal experience of taking tranquillisers and the deaths of two male peer acquaintances.

They're just not good for you. You don't know what they do to your insides, you don't know what your stomach's taking in. I mean fair enough people are prescribed them, but I mean it's probably like take one every eight hours or something, but people are necking like five. Also . . . I didn't really want to get in to this but anyway. Two people who I've known for years are dead now because of wobblies. It was Phil's funeral on Friday, it blew my mind totally. They died within weeks of each other. Both of them had been on wobblies and E, and both of them choked on their own vomit when they were asleep. It's just not good. Pills you just don't touch them. That's me like – no pills for me.

Emily continues to move in social circles where all street drugs are available including heroin and, of course, ecstasy.

Well round about November before Christmas, Lulu had some E. She got me one, she was – 'Look what I got you.' I went – 'You daft cunt.' And that was the only thing I said to her. She went – 'I guess you don't want one then?' I just ignored her. She done the same thing with wobblies. A couple of years back, when I was about thirteen, I OD'ed and had to get my stomach pumped. After that I was like – 'no tablets for me, take them away'. She knows that. I just said to her – 'If you're a pal, don't do that again', and she hasn't. I know that I can resist the temptation but I don't want to be tempted, I don't want anybody to come and put pills in my face. I don't want anything to do with that kind of thing.

Our respondent felt in control of her drug use and accepted full responsibility for her own actions.

I just wish there wasn't a stigma that cannabis leads to harder drugs, because it doesn't. It hasn't with me. I haven't went out intentionally and thought – I need a better buzz, I need to try something bigger, harder. I hate the fact that you see kids, aged twelve, wobbled off their faces wandering about, just because they think it's big in front of their pals. I hate that. If you're going to take drugs, you're going to take it because you want to, not because you've got peer pressure, not because everybody else is, because you want to, you want to experience it, not because you want to fit in.'

She felt her drug use was reducing slightly because of the influence of her boyfriend and her responsibilities as a student and also simply a lack of money.

I think if I had more money, I think I would just buy more tack. I don't think I'd be more reckless. I think I'd still be . . . I'd probably sit up on a Friday night . . . I'd probably get Lulu round here with Tom because I don't usually see Tom. I probably just get them in here and sit and have an all-nighter, but I haven't got the money for that, because you get to half past twelve and you got no tack left. If I didn't have work, I think if I was getting like seventy–eighty pound dole every two weeks, and I didn't have a job or anything to get up for, I think I'd be monged, I think I'd get money from somewhere. But that's not the way it is. I know I've got to work to the end of my NVQ, I've got to watch what I'm doing, I've got to cut back on my drug abuse. I got to be sensible, I'm getting older now, I'm coming up to my seventeenth birthday, so I get a little bit of a pay rise. I've just got to be sensible and watch what I'm doing, and live up to my responsibilities.

However she also noted her tendency to take risks in certain settings and that some of her drug initiation was in the weekend 'night out mode' whereby:

I think if I was going out and I was drunk, and somebody went – 'There's an E for you.' I think I'd probably go – 'Oh what the hell', and take it. I don't want to do that. If I had my brain I would say no, but when you're out you don't know what's going on do you. (142004 female, drug user, 17 yrs)

This young woman illustrates how a recreational drugs career can develop: shaped by drugs availability, the impact of peer networks, close relationships, alcoholic social settings and occupational/educational goals and priorities. Currently 'bounded' by a conventional boyfriend and the need to do well on her NVQ (further training) course and her own notions of sensible drug use, this interviewee also enjoyed her drug use, her nights out and 'time out'. She is well aware of the 'temptations' that are inherent in her current hedonistic social life and the tendency for misjudgements to be made in these settings. Her future drugs career is likely to be shaped by new contingencies as she leaves further education or changes her social network. She seems unlikely to give up all drug use in the near future however.

Becoming a Problem Drug User

In Chapter 6 we describe how a very small minority of young people, who invariably begin with the early drinking, drug trying episodes, as described by this sample, become involved with heroin as triers and then users. We argue that young heroin users in this new decade will be found not just among socially deprived and excluded 'vulnerable' populations, but also as rare but very real casualties of the recreational scene. We finish this qualitative analysis with an uncomfortable exemplar of one young woman whose 'early onset' of drug trying found her out. An archetypal, intelligent, outgoing early risk taker, this middle-class young woman annually talked enthusiastically about her drug use, particularly her enjoyment of cannabis and LSD. At 15 she was already in the club scene through older boyfriends, claiming to be *drugwise* and sensible.

> Because I was with my boyfriend and he was upstairs (in a night-club)....One of the lasses comes up to me and she said 'do you want some smack. It makes you feel beautiful, it makes you feel mint, it makes you feel proper high up.' But I didn't want to try it because it's sure bad for you. I've always thought steer well clear of E and stay well clear of heroin and stay well clear of crack. They're just too bad for you. I know the risks with cannabis and LSD . . . but they are accepted.

A year later and after many nights of ecstasy this young woman was also becoming a regular heroin user. Her fascination with the club scene and her associations with older men provided too many opportunities to try heroin. At age 16 she felt she could take it or leave it:

> Once you've done heroin you don't see it as such a big thing. People who haven't done it they see it as a big . . . wow heroin! But after you've done it it's like well, it's just a smoke.

At 17 she had built up numerous heroin contacts and while she remained located in a middle-class world of home, Saturday job and sixth form education, her other subcultural world was always calling from the housing estate at the other end of town.

> The people at the flats, I wouldn't say that they were my friends to be honest. They're associates who I take drugs with. There's one guy down there who I do really get on with. We always take . . . well most of the time we take drugs when we're with each other. I mean we are best friends, anyone who ever looks at me funny, he's like in their face. We get on really well, but at the end of the day if I didn't take drugs, then I wouldn't go down there as much and I wouldn't. . . . I mean there's that closeness when you take heroin with someone but only while the heroin lasts. Just heroin partners.

Within this world she has met and become associated with well organised local level dealers.

> I bought some brown on Thursday, and the guy I bought it off, after me moaning – 'No I want more brown than that, and by the way I'm doing it at your house.' He got out these tablets, he was showing me these methadone tablets, and I just said – 'Give me one.' So he just gave me a couple of these methadone tablets.

And up the line of command

> Actually there was one guy, I used to hang around with him when we were younger. I started to hang round with him again, and he was dealing small time. Then he started dealing big time for the main guy, and I didn't get on with him after that. But the main guy, he was supposed to come to Alton Towers with me on Sunday, but he didn't because he didn't wake up the lazy bastard. But it's like I get on with the main guy better than the guys who deal for him. He doesn't do it himself, the main guy, he doesn't smoke it. If you saw him, you'd just think – 'ordinary guy', but he is actually pretty big in the druggy and gangster world.
> [*How do you know him?*]
> It was really weird actually. I was in a club, and he come up to me, and he said something like – 'Oh god you're dead fit, I'd love to fuck you.' He said – 'Look I'll be honest, I don't even want to know your name, I just think we should have sex.' I ended up necking on with

him, I was on ecstasy. A couple of months later, after I didn't ring him, how did I meet him again? That was it, there was a guy who was dealing, and he used to give to me free, that's how I got back into it, because he fancied me. He used to give me a bag a day for nothing. When it's coming free, your addiction just goes through the roof. (292050 female, 17 yrs)

Conclusion

Drugs decision making continues right through adolescence and, as we shall see in Chapter 5, on into young adulthood. Qualitative studies, if well conducted, allow us to understand the nature of these assessments and how conclusions, however temporary, are reached. The journeys we have described are immensely complex and the whole process is dynamic throughout. For some, the early risk takers, beginning to understand and explore illicit drugs scenes and starting to become *drugwise* occurs alongside moving to secondary school (McKeganey, 1999). For others, who steadfastly maintain their abstinence throughout adolescence and attempt to avoid all drugs encounters, their drugs wisdom is more focused on saying no. As we have shown drugs initiation can occur at any stage of adolescence depending on a variety of factors, from availability to the impact of friendship networks, to the contingencies of a particular social scene most notably, at around age 17, being part of serious nights out in town, going out with friends in party mode. This complexity and dynamism, plus the rational, consumerist, hedonistic approach to decision making by young people are still processes which are rarely grasped in public debates about 'preventing' people taking drugs.

It may well be that the failure or only marginal success of the 1980s–90s 'PSE' drugs prevention programmes (Brown and Kreft, 1998; Dorn and Murji, 1992; White and Pitts, 1998) is because they have neither understood nor tuned into how young people become *drugwise* and have thus been over ambitious in their aspirational goals. Unfortunately while abstainers and former triers tend to approve of and gain reinforcement from primary prevention 'say no' programmes, we, by definition, find much greater scepticism and less impact amongst drug triers and users who tend to pick and choose what information they take on board. This is now a critical problem because we are identifying weaknesses and inadequacies in young people's knowledge base particularly in respect of heroin and cocaine. Alas this is in part at least an unintentional outcome of the 'one pill can kill' demonising messages they have had about, for instance, the dangers of ecstasy. The younger cohort in the surveys discussed in the last chapter rated ecstasy as *more* dangerous than heroin.

This only adds to the complexity. Not only is drugs wisdom affected by region and by age and maturity across adolescence, but it is reconstructed within different age cohorts. What the year 8s think is not the same as the year 11s think, but is not anyway the same as what the year 11s thought when they were 13 (year 8s). This is not an academic nicety. It is a crucial factor which we need to take account of in ensuring each age wave of young people have sufficient, accurate information to make informed drugs decisions which take account of their local drugs scene as they are experiencing it. This is another reason for developing accurate monitoring of local drugs scenes (see Chapter 8).

If the national strategy is serious about reducing the number of young people using drugs, and particularly 'harder' drugs like heroin and cocaine, then it is not the committed abstainers but adolescent recreational drug triers and users who should be targeted given that they have been unmoved by school based prevention programmes. However, if we are to engage them then it will need to be far more on their terms and through their modes of observing, conversing and learning about street drugs. The drug journeys we have described and young people's utilization of the cost–benefit assessment suggest that drug triers and users want to stay safe and attempt to use illicit drugs in ways which minimize mishap and problems with use and avoid 'dangerous' drugs altogether. Clearly they make mistakes and in disinhibited moments cross self imposed boundaries. Nevertheless, in the absence of routine help from the state by way of secondary prevention, harm reductive and public health information, young drug triers and users have constructed a basic knowledge illustrated in the cost–benefit formula. It distinguishes between drugs by desired effect, risk and side effects but is, in the UK, currently based primarily on knowledge about cannabis and the dance drugs because these have been the most widely available and used drugs of the 1990s. There is little doubt that in respect of more addictive drugs whether physically (heroin) or psychologically (cocaine/crack cocaine) youthful drugs wisdom is less sophisticated and complete – a theme we shall explore fully in later chapters when we look at the 'casualty rate' of young people who become heavily involved with these drugs.

5

Unstoppable? Dance Drug Use in the UK Club Scene

Fiona Measham, Judith Aldridge and Howard Parker

Purpose

As the first generation of drug using and drug experienced 1990s youth move into adulthood, a key research and policy question must be – will they settle down and leave drug use behind them, or 'carry over' their recreational drug use as the new twentysomething population? In this chapter we summarise the findings of the largest UK study to date of drug use in the nightclub/dance club scene. We find a very drug experienced population on the dance floor. Their drugs histories and pathways from adolescence, plus their current alcohol–poly drug repertoires, make them, by any measure, very drug involved. They are undoubtedly at the most serious end of recreational drug use.

The dance drug users do report some health costs and problems, and occasional concerns about personal safety and security, but they consider these to be 'sufferable' and acceptable consequences of their nights out. They continue to say a conditional yes to drugs.

The conundrum for the state is multi-faceted. There is widespread disregard for the law and Class A drugs are involved. That such defiance comes from a largely well educated, employed, otherwise conventional twentysomething population is no comfort to a national strategy committed to radically reducing drug use. Indeed, given that the clubbers have rejected prevention messages and are unlikely to appear as 'problem' users in either of the two main 'capture' systems – the criminal justice system and/or treatment services – the UK drugs strategy is short on ideas.

The official backstop position is enforcement yet, in practice, there is no political or strategic will to close down all nightclubs or prosecute the dance drug users. While this pragmatic nonintervention shows realism, it exposes the contradictions at the heart of official thinking about drug use *per se*, compared with drug use which generates dependency and acquisitive crime.

The Going Out, Time Out Population

The time is long gone when a specific group, in this case dance drug users, can be described in subcultural terms (Merchant and Macdonald, 1994; Sumner, 1994). With estimates of up to one million ecstasy tablets being consumed each week in the UK (POST, 1996) and leisure industry data suggesting that one-in-two under 24 year olds frequently visit the UK's 4000 licensed clubs and discos, we must count dance drug users in units of hundreds of thousands given that there are over 15 million visits to nightclubs a year (Finch, 1999). Dance drug use must instead be seen as an accommodated part of the leisure sector which probably involves attendance by the majority of British young adults.

Going out 'on the town' drinking with friends has a long and distinguished tradition in the UK as in many other European countries (Calafat, 1998). In Chapter 4 we described the entry into this social world at around age 17. There have long been variations on this theme with self selecting minorities favouring dancing from the beginning of the last century (Kohn, 1997). The arrival of ecstasy in the late 1980s and its immediate links with an electronic 'DJ' led type of 'mixed' dance music saw the development of another genre. However the decade of dance (1988–98) would not have reached the significance it did during the 1990s without the widespread accommodation of drug use into time out adventures. At the new millennium the consumption of stimulant and hallucinogenic drugs like amphetamines, cocaine, LSD, ketamine and especially ecstasy has become widespread within the going out population of post adolescents and twentysomethings. However while drug use has actually replaced alcohol for a minority of dance club devotees, in describing the overall scene we should still see alcohol as the backbone of weekend time out. This is because it is licensed premises – the pubs, bars, café bars and clubs – which provide the 'circuits' and venues for socialising, serving up the main psycho-active drug – alcohol. Illicit drug use is becoming more prevalent in this time out sector while within the dance club–nightclub element of this industry it is already endemic.

Profiles of the Clubbing Population

The accommodation of dance drug use in the going out scenes has been Europe wide (Calafat, 1998). However in some countries, for example

Finland and France, this is marginal while in others, for instance Germany, Italy and Denmark, there is an identifiable dance drug–dance club scene. The Netherlands, although its youth population is generally far less drug involved than in the UK, has a vibrant clubber–party goer scene. In its party venues it is routine to find a very drug experienced customer base, whereby around 80 per cent will have used ecstasy and two thirds amphetamines (for example Van de Wijngaart *et al.*, 1998).

Once again, however, when we compare the UK with other European countries the remarkable feature is that British youth and twentysome-things are far more drug experienced than elsewhere. In relation to 'synthetic' drug use – amphetamines, LSD and ecstasy – the UK heads the European comparative league tables, having lifetime and past year rates over twice as high as the next placed country and roughly three times the rates of the rest (Griffiths *et al.*, 1997).

This picture is reinforced when we look at the clutch of UK surveys and case studies of the dance drug–nightclub scene. A reader survey of over 4000 regular clubbers by *Mix-Mag* (Petridis, 1996) found 81 per cent were current and regular ecstasy users, while another survey of 496 dance event attendees (Release, 1997) found lifetime rates of well over 80 per cent for cannabis, LSD, amphetamines and ecstasy and cocaine at 62 per cent. This survey also noted that the clubbers were predomi-nantly 15–30 year olds and from all social backgrounds but with a strong presence from people in further and higher education. The sample had a distinctive pick 'n' mix approach to drug use combining alcohol with illicit drugs but nominating ecstasy as their favourite drug to go out dancing 'with'.

Forsyth (1996; 1998) undertook a case study interviewing 135 'ravers' who had attended nightclubs in the west end of Glasgow. Their average age was 24 and 70 per cent were in their twenties. Most were frequent drinkers, tobacco smokers and drug users, especially of cannabis. Over 90 per cent had 'ever tried' amphetamines, LSD and ecstasy and in fact these rates were nearly as high for past year use. Even for cocaine 59 per cent had a past year experience.

A linked study, conducted at the same time though published much later (Hammersley *et al.*, 1999), made important points about ecstasy being part of poly-drug use repertoires. This particular study utilizing a chain referral approach to sampling ecstasy users also found quite high rates of self reported delinquency in the lifestyles of this particular sample. A case study in Nottingham (Akram and Galt, 1999) produced very similar results, again based on off-site interviews with 125 dance drug users and with even higher cocaine take up. Interviews with 98 ecstasy users (mean age 25 years) in Northern Ireland (McElrath and McEvoy, 1999) reinforced this general profile again finding very sophisticated drugs careers revolving around stimulant drugs alongside the 'ubiquitous' cannabis. With other case studies in Wales (Handy *et al.*, 1998) and Manchester (Sherlock in Calafat, 1998) reaching similar conclusions we can be fairly confident that clubbers right across the UK have similar profiles.

The clubbers who dance on drugs have extensive drugs experience, which alongside their alcohol and tobacco use, puts them at the serious end of the UK recreational drug scenes. They are poly drug users who choose different drugs, licit and illicit, and combinations to produce specific effects and moods. What is also clear is that they are post adolescents and twentysomethings and come disproportionately from higher social groups. They are usually either in higher education or employment. Overall they are not a particularly delinquent or criminal group.

Upon this backcloth we now summarize some of the findings of a large-scale dance club–nightclub study in north west England.

The Nightclub Fieldwork

There is little prospect of a nightclub study, which can claim to be representative of the diversity found in the UK's 4000 plus nightclubs/dance clubs, that cover so many niche markets and musical styles. In this investigation the focus was on dance club venues, which, by playing dance music (as in house, techno, hardcore, old skool and so forth) attracted a post adolescent and twentysomething customer base. The main aims of the investigation were:

- to profile dance club customers
- to estimate the prevalence of alcohol and dance drug use in clubs
- to assess the health implications of short and long term dance drug use
- to explore the safety agenda, management and policing of clubs.

The three clubs were all found in north west England. The Warehouse club was found on the edge of the city centre. It played a whole variety of dance music hosted by national DJs. Transformation was an out-of-town leisure centre which metamorphosised into a large scale Saturday night multi arena, hardcore rave type dance event. Otherside was a city centre multi-level 'house' club with a strong gay and lesbian customer base, particularly at weekends. All these clubs had a large capacity ranging from several hundred to over 5000.

The research team was made up of 12 interviewers, all with established interviewing skills and a 'clubbing' background. One was a male nurse who also supervised the on site 'medicals'. Much effort went into training, team building and continuous feedback to the fieldworkers about progress and procedures. There were 21 long fieldwork nights and in each club the SPARC workstation was set up near the entrance to the club or in another suitable thoroughfare. Interview 'sites' within each club were also identified where the music decibels were less intrusive and some privacy afforded.

In order to profile the customers of each club on each fieldwork night a major 'sweep' survey took place, in which each interviewer undertook numerous two to four minute interviews with people as, or just after, they entered the club. This involved operating a basic quota sampling system of 1:1 males:females and 9:1 white:black/Asian, and operating the sweep across the fieldwork night so as to represent late comers as well as early queuers. However, given the massive activity on some nights and a significantly higher refusal rate by Asian customers, pushing the overall refusal rate to 6 per cent, we should not pretend that this quota sampling was fully achieved, nor that we have a sample representative of anything more than the customer base of the chosen venues. This said we have produced the largest sample of clubbers so far and arguably the most detailed 'in club' independent academic UK study conducted.

Figure 5.1 provides an overview of the research design and 'flow'. Over the 21 fieldwork nights 2057 customers undertook brief interviews packed with questions about their drug and alcohol consumption and basic profiles ranging from employment to sexual orientation. This provides us with the alcohol and/or drugs consumption rates for the clubbers in three venues over 21 nights. From this sample we selected our *dance drug sample*. For selection, respondents had a dance drug use history which was defined as: having taken one or more of LSD, amphetamines, ecstasy, cocaine or crack in the last three months and also on the fieldwork night. This sample was built up by each interviewer 'tracking' volunteers across the night, undertaking a detailed interview lasting about 30 minutes at an agreed time and meeting point, and also guiding the 'clubber' to the workstation. Here the nurse would take pulse, temperature, pupil dilation measures, mood and intoxication assessments and organise a urine sample. A *comparison sample* was also identified during the sweep, whereby we undertook full interviews with customers who were

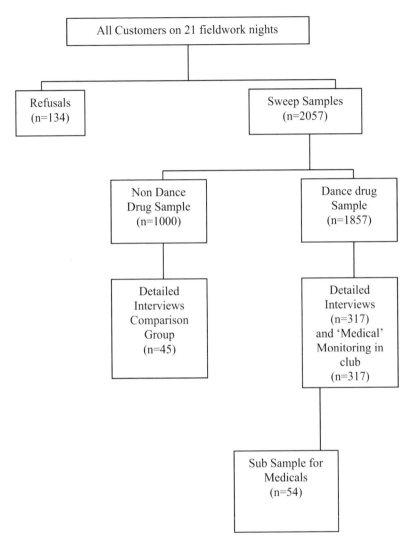

Figure 5.1 Interviewing and assessing the clubbers: overview and flow

not taking dance drugs on the fieldwork night and had not taken dance drugs within the last year.

Finally from the dance drug sample we developed a further sub-sample to complete a half day medical assessment at a university medical facility. Here a wide range of physical and psychological assessments were undertaken including blood tests. The main purpose of these tests was to check for any morbidity which might be associated with regular dance drug use.

It should be noted that an enormous number of negotiations and protocols were involved in this study, including Medical Ethics Committees, arrangements with the police, negotiations with club management and an elaborate set of personal safety measures for the fieldwork staff. Remarkably, aside from some spilt urine, a very last minute cancellation of a club night at one venue and occasional challenges from clubbers as to our purpose and sexual orientation, the whole fieldwork process ran smoothly and without incident.

In this summary, for some results from the study we will refer to the sweep or club sample (n = 2057) and to the interview sample (n = 362) when we combine results from the dance drug users' and comparison respondents.

The Clubbers' Nights Out

Who are they?

Table 5.1 presents a summary of the demographic characteristics of the customer base of the three clubs. The higher proportion of males, despite our quota sampling approach, does accurately reflect the disproportionate presence particularly of white males in these venues. Although the age range was from 15–57 the mean age of 23 and median of 21 is important: clubbers who dance to dance music are predominantly in their early to mid twenties. Another key finding is that such clubbers are predominantly employed or in education and training. They are not unemployed or dislocated from institutional arrangements, instead being or becoming productive citizens. There will be clubs attracting a more excluded profile, but both this and previous studies suggest that clubbers most frequently come from the higher and middle socio-economic groups and the 'working' working classes.

Alcohol and tobacco use

As expected the clubbers, quite aside from their propensity for illicit drug use, are also experienced tobacco and alcohol users. Sixty eight per cent of the club sample (n = 2057) were current smokers and 96 per cent current drinkers with three-quarters drinking twice or more each week – much higher rates than the norm even in their age group.

On the night they were interviewed the mean number of alcohol units already consumed before club entry was eight with an anticipated

Table 5.1   Demographic characteristics of the clubbers (n = 2057) %

Mean age 23 yrs	range 15–57
♦ Female 45	Male 55
♦ White 94	Black 3
♦ Asian 2	Other 1
♦ Straight 77	Gay/lesbian 18
♦ Bisexual 6	
♦ Full-time employed 58	
♦ Higher education 24	
♦ Unemployed 6	

further six units to be drunk. In short, the night out begins earlier in the evening for most clubbers as they first sample the night out–bar circuit scene, though not for Transformation customers to the same extent because of its out-of-town location and more hardcore non-drinking rave crowd. The overall picture on these fieldwork nights is of 78 per cent of the overall sample (n = 2057) having already had alcohol before entering the club and of 84 per cent having had alcohol by the end of their night out. Alcohol remains the key psycho-active substance for nearly all clubbers but for most it is supplemented with drugs.

The essential mix: alcohol and drugs

With only 4 per cent of the clubbers consuming neither alcohol nor illicit drugs, the basic picture on each fieldwork night is of the vast major-ity of customers arriving at their venue already well into their psycho-active consumption. Of the 84 per cent who were drinking, 63 per cent of these had already or planned to take at least one drug on the night. Of the 64 per cent of the club sample who had already or planned to take at least one drug, 82 per cent had already been or planned to drink alcohol. In short whichever way we approach it we find the mixing of alcohol and drugs is the most common approach to psycho-active con-sumption (see Figure 5.2).

Turning to the drugs involved Table 5.2 lists the drugs taken or to be taken by two-thirds of the club sample disclosing drug use. Leaving aside cannabis, we can see that the two most significant drugs were amphet-amines and ecstasy – still the staple stimulant diet of clubbers right across the 1990s. While cocaine use is growing in the club scene and among the going out sector and despite 45 per cent of the sample having used cocaine (27 per cent in past three months), it is not a dance club

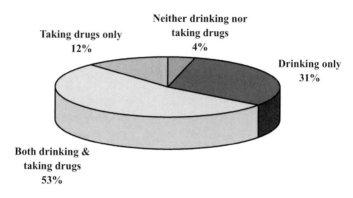

Figure 5.2   The essential mix

favourite. The sample nominated ecstasy (78 per cent), amphetamines (64 per cent), cannabis (16 per cent) before cocaine (11 per cent) as their 'favourite drug to take when clubbing'.

Aside from poppers, the other drugs consumed are almost certainly related to users' general drugs consumption rather than specifically because they are out clubbing. The ubiquitous cannabis, although the most used drug on the night out, is clearly not a favourite in respect of being on the dance floor. It's generalist role includes being smoked during the day and while getting ready to go out and being used as the essential 'chill out' drug in particular to help bring people down, relax and eventually get to sleep as part of the recovery period. This generic role distinguishes cannabis from the main dance drugs. Asked about

Table 5.2

Q: Had (or planning to); drug taking on fieldwork night (n = 2057) %	
♦ *At least one*	65
♦ Cannabis	42
♦ Ecstasy	36
♦ Amphetamines	32
♦ Poppers	9
♦ Cocaine	7
♦ LSD	2
♦ Tranquillisers	< 1
♦ GHB	< 1
♦ Crack	< 1
♦ Heroin	< 1
♦ Viagra	< 1

their favourite drugs and combination for an ideal night out clubbing, the club sample concluded that if they did use stimulant drugs the ideal timing would be thus:

ecstasy	44 per cent before, 63 per cent inside the dance club, 9 per cent after the event;
amphetamines	73 per cent before, 31 per cent inside the dance club, 4 per cent after the event;
cocaine	61 per cent before, 43 per cent inside the dance club, 2 per cent after the event.

Whereas for cannabis the ratios were ideally 58 per cent before, only 12 per cent at the venue but 85 per cent after the event, illustrating its post-club 'chill out' function.

Our typical clubber's essential mix, alongside the cigarettes, involves some drug use leading up to and perhaps during the early part of their night out, steady drinking across the evening before preparing for the dance venue by taking a stimulant drug (often amphetamine) and perhaps topping up with drugs inside the venue, continuing to drink and saving the cannabis for the end of the night out and, thus, final 'depressant' drug dosing. For the clubbers whatever variations on the theme of combining the licit with the illicit, the stimulant with the depressant, the powders, pills and plants, they all find it essential to mix.

The Cost of Clubbing

With 83 per cent of the interview sample defining themselves as regular clubbers and nearly half (47 per cent) going clubbing at least once a week, spending over £50 (mean) in total on each night out and £18 (mean) on their drugs, the financial costs of clubbing are considerable. But are there other costs? In this section we look at the potential down-sides of dancing on drugs in respect of the need to recover physically and mentally plus any negative effects on personal health and fears about personal safety.

Recovering

After a very long night out travelling, bar drinking, spending several hours in the club often dancing for long periods routinely sustained by stimulant drugs, going on to another setting or getting home, clubbers require a recovery period. With nearly all this sample in full-time employment or higher education this recovery period is perhaps shaped

Table 5.3   'Recovery' after clubbing drug use (n = 362)

- ♦ Self-reported length of time taken to 'recover' from drug use after clubbing
  - mean 1.72 days
  - mode 1 day
- ♦ Drug use affecting 'week after'
  - 58% no effect
  - 13% affects 'performance'
  - 12% tired
  - 8% absent/late from work
  - 7% concentration/memory loss
  - 7% mood swings
  - 2% improves work performance

---

by the need to use one, sometimes two, weekend days to recuperate. The most quoted period was a day (the mode) but the mean was 1.7 days with a range of one to seven days.

In relation to the effects of excessive weekends on the week after, Table 5.3 describes the range of negative effects. Clearly the majority (58 per cent) perceived their immediate recovery slot as adequate to return to normal functioning. However over four in ten indicated that there were costs. These all broadly relate to performance deficits, whereby feeling tired, anxious or 'moody' meant being less able to keep schedules and be focused, both work wise and in terms of maintaining effective social relationships.

Self reported health costs and self regulation

Focusing still on the interview sample we asked them if they had experienced any problems with their health or well being that they thought was caused by drugs and/or alcohol, remembering that for the majority nights out involved combining the two. Almost half (48 per cent) felt they had. These revolved around appetite problems, weight loss, depression and lung/chest problems (see also Williamson *et al.*, 1997).

Nearly a quarter of the interview sample (23 per cent) had consulted a doctor in respect of health problems they associated with alcohol/drug use and 11 per cent had been seen by paramedics/first aid staff at some time in their clubbing career. When asked if they had ever been seen at an Accident and Emergency Department (ER) as a result of drugs/clubbing, 11 per cent said they had been to Casualty as a result of drug use. This is a surprisingly high figure but will undoubtedly include the consequences of mixing drugs and combining alcohol and drugs.

One of the unexpected and, scientifically, unforeseen characteristics of the comparison sample (n = 45) was that while they did not fit our regular current dance drug user criteria they did not fit our clubbers who don't take drugs 'ideal' either. They often turned out to be very experienced dance drug users who had 'given up', or were resting, or self enforcing a period of abstinence. Indeed the majority of the main current dance drug sample had also employed self regulatory tactics whereby 85 per cent of the overall interview sample had cut down or stopped using certain drugs. Interestingly speed (amphetamines) was most often rationed (45 per cent) followed by ecstasy (31 per cent), cannabis (19 per cent) and cocaine (5 per cent). Indeed speed was nominated by 30 per cent (of the 48 per cent of the interview sample who identified problems) followed by 'all drugs' (24 per cent), alcohol (12 per cent) and ecstasy (11 per cent) as the drug most likely to be perceived as having caused health problems.

Personal safety and security

There is no doubt that young adults, particularly males, who go out to town or city centre a lot are particularly likely to be victims of crime or assault (HMSO 1999). Indeed 21 per cent of the interview sample had at some time been admitted to an Accident and Emergency Department for an injury sustained while out pubbing or clubbing. These range from falling over, glass or bottle injuries, being pushed or hit or involved in a fight. Moreover 53 per cent agreed that at some stage in their career they had felt threatened, intimidated or harassed specifically in the club setting. They nominated other clubbers (50 per cent), club, mainly security, staff (42 per cent), the police (20 per cent outside plus 9 per cent inside) and drug dealers (14 per cent) as the catalysts or 'perpetrators'. Yet despite all this our respondents were philosophical. Their dominant response to questions about how safe they usually felt in clubland was 'very safe' (4.3 out of 5 on a 1–5 scale).

The final security issue for clubbers is how to get home in the early hours, often with no public transport facilities available. The majority of clubbers in this study took taxis home, although our observation was that 'fighting' over taxis was an unintended consequence of this sensible strategy. However, 28 per cent of clubbers were driven home by friends and 19 per cent drove themselves home. That nearly half these often alcohol affected/'drugged up' or very tired clubbers use private cars, usually containing companions, while 4 per cent catch a night bus, is not only a safety/security issue for them but also for other members of the public (Automobile Association, 1998).

Table 5.4 Prevalence of selected drugs (n = 2057) %

	Lifetime	3 months
◆ *At least one*	94	84
◆ Cannabis	87	70
◆ Amphetamines	77	54
◆ Poppers	72	30
◆ Ecstasy	67	51
◆ LSD	52	15
◆ Cocaine	45	27
◆ Tranquillisers	15	6
◆ GHB	11	6
◆ Crack	7	2
◆ Heroin	6	2
◆ Viagra	3	2

Pathways to Regular Dance Drug Use

It is important to look for any clues as to how such a determined group of serious recreational drug users is created. There is a significant gap between the rates of adolescent drug use we described in Chapters 1 and 3 and these twentysomething clubbers' drugs consumption. We have noted a major shortfall in our knowledge about the way adolescents become or remain drug involved. Young Britons are 'lost', research wise, when they leave school where surveys can be administered. While we do have a handful of higher education student studies and the private household survey 'basic' measures, these cannot plug all the gaps.

Unfortunately this research could not, in a survey slot of 2–4 minutes, produce detailed drugs histories but we did collect some chronological drugs trying and use data. First, the transition period between the onset of nights out – circuit drinking at around age 17 (Chapter 4) and starting clubbing is, for many, very short. Second, most of the clubbers seem to have the classic early risk taker characteristics and the smoking and drinking markers that so many studies have identified as predictive of later regular drug use (for example Goddard and Higgins, 1999; Parker *et al.*, 1998). Third, they have tended to pass through similar drugs trying gateways. In Table 5.4, based on the large club sweep sample, we can see how drug experienced they are both in terms of ever trying so many drugs and sustaining use. However if we look at the order of initiation (Table 5.5) or how long ago they first tried illicit drugs, and remembering their mean age of 23, we can see that their drugs careers started in early to mid adolscence. Here we see the same starting and

Table 5.5   Drugs careers: number of years since
first taking the main illicit drugs (n = 2057)

	Years
Solvents	10.4
Cannabis	8.1
Fresh mushrooms	7.4
Dried mushrooms	7.3
LSD	6.8
Heroin	6.4
Poppers	6.2
Barbiturates	6.2
Amphetamines	5.9
Methadone	5.8
Opium	5.6
Ecstasy	4.7
Tranquillisers	4.3
Others	4.3
Anabolic steroids	4.2
Legal herbal highs	3.6
Ketamine	3.5
Cocaine	3.3
Crack	3.1
GHB	1.3
Viagra	0.0

trying patterns routinely identified in studies of 1990s adolescents beginning with solvents/gases then cannabis with the trying of LSD, poppers and amphetamines in mid adolescence and the later onset of ecstasy and cocaine almost certainly in parallel to joining the party–going out scene from around age 17–18. The other drugs, although included in the chronological list, are far less likely to have been tried or used (see Table 5.4).

Discussion

Despite the high levels of drug use generated by the club samples at our three dance club–nightclub venues, these rates were somewhat lower than those found in the other studies undertaken during the mid 1990s, almost certainly because we chose large scale, dance music venues and tried to sample and estimate drug use in the whole customer base. Nevertheless, the pick 'n' mix approach to alcohol, stimulant and depressant drugs found in most qualitative studies (for example, Boys *et al.*, 1998; Hammersley *et al.*, 1999; Parker *et al.*, 1998; Release, 1997;

Shewan *et al.*, 2000) once again stands out. There is a strong rational consumerist approach to the way clubbers and, indeed, most recreational drug users make drugs decisions. The cost–benefit framework adolescent drug users attempt to operate, which we described in Chapter 4, is seen here in full flow. The dance drug users have very clear ideas about which drugs to use, where, when and for what specific benefits or functions. They seamlessly combine the licit, their tobacco and alcohol, with their generalist most used illicit drug, cannabis, saving their stimulant drugs, amphetamines, ecstasy and cocaine, for 'time out' energy and intoxicated well being. They learn through experience, some of it bad, to reduce or stop taking certain drugs or combinations. They recognize and accept the immediate price of psycho-active weekends and so build in recovery time. Their assessment of longer term consequences is less well developed.

There are many other similarities with the adolescent drug users. The clubbers also 'sort' drugs out for each other and use regular, known sources of drugs supply (see Chapter 2). They too try to keep their distance from 'real' drug dealers and, despite the media stereotypes, most are not likely to buy drugs from strangers or dealers in clubland certainly by preference. All this prompts the question – are we seeing the multi-dimensional normalisation of adolescent recreational drug use (Parker *et al.*, 1998) being carried over into adult life? We have shown how the clubbers are largely migrants from adolescent drug use. For most their serious drugs experience began in their mid teens and most of today's clubbers were adolescents in the last decade.

An impressive case can be made for this conclusion: the gradual age extension of normalisation. The clubbers cannot be pathologised as underclass losers or a subcultural, deviant minority. They are largely productive, conforming citizens (Release, 1997). Their drug trying and drug use rates are unequivocally high and on-going. They have no difficulty obtaining their drugs through normal and normative social relationships. They blur the licit and illicit. They use a consumerist, risk assessment approach to drugs decisions and are clearly comfortable with their drugs status and, indeed, show immense commitment to their drugs consumption if we consider the costs they endure. One in five has been cautioned/convicted of a drugs offence, they have suffered a range of negatives from comedowns to Casualty visits, yet they continue their drug use, sustained if necessary, by resting or revising their drugs repertoires. They are, in many ways, model, postmodern, 'risk society' citizens.

On the other hand, we may be better viewing the night clubbers as, by being at the most serious end of recreational drug use, just a little too hedonistic and excessive to be accommodated by their non (or cautious) drug using twentysomething peers. Certainly within clubland they socialise and dance side by side with those only drinking alcohol and their behaviour is tolerated, even condoned, by the management and staff of the licensed premises they frequent. However, could we really see them openly discussing or imbibing the amounts of different drugs they do on weekend nights in other social settings beyond time out venues? The nightclub allows serious recreational drug users to come together and 'share' their dance drug use which anyway loses much of its 'brilliance' in the absence of the music, the crowds and collective dis-inhibition. Put another way the nightclub contains, even segregates, the dance drug users. It also acts as an initiation venue for newcomers.

For these reasons we cannot quite fit the clubbers into the normal-isation thesis we developed in respect of 'sensible' recreational drug use based on our longitudinal studies of adolescents. There are many factors and features consistent with normalisation and no major contraindica-tors but at the same time the clubbers' drug use remains atypical and rather situationally specific and segregated. We still need more research knowledge about drug use among a wider range of twentysomethings and in more generic social settings before conclusions can be reached about whether widespread drug trying and use, and its social accom-modation which occurs within youth culture, will extend into adult lifestyles.

Turning now to the 'political' implications of dance drug use by the going out–clubland population, we can see some uncomfortable contra-dictions emerging. The national drugs strategy targets Class A drug use seeking significant reductions in the use of such drugs. However, it officially assumes the taking of such drugs becomes associated with problematic drug use and ill health, eventually requiring treatment interventions and/or pulls such drug users into other offending, hence the overarching emphasis and investment in criminal justice and prison based interventions (Cabinet Office, 1999).

The clubbers and going out sector – and there are hundreds of thou-sands of them in the UK – take a lot of drugs including Class A ecstasy and cocaine. Technically they supply each other Class A drugs, with 91 per cent of the interview sample having received illegal drugs from friends and 78 per cent admitting giving or selling drugs to friends. Although demonstrating defiance and disrespect for the law is not their aim, this the clubbers do quite comprehensively and in semi public, licensed, inspected premises. However, because of their social profiles and self regulated drug use very few, except by chance or neglect, are likely to be caught up in the criminal justice system beyond personal possession. The health agenda is more complex. We clearly have had some fatalities but these are small in relation to the proportion of users. More widespread is the cluster of problems with physical and psychological health and the (unclear) effects of long-term 'mixing' of alcohol and drugs which increases toxicity (Winstock, 2000). The rates of self reported problems alongside the scale of consultation with doctors and rates of emergency interventions suggest there is a price to be paid for dancing on drugs. In many ways the demonising of ecstasy seems irrelevant in this world of poly drug use and recommendations that ecstasy be reclassified to 'Class B' seem increasingly realistic (for example, Hammersley *et al.*, 1999; Independent Inquiry, 2000).

The UK drugs strategy simply runs out of ideas for this drugs reality. It offers no harm reduction initiatives and no proactive programmes for this group. Where these occur they are locally designed and delivered (Branigan *et al.*, 1997). Indeed it assumes that post 25 year olds have settled down. The official fall back position is enforcement. Drug use is wrong and illegal and thus nightclubs must, if necessary, be closed down. The 1997 Public Entertainment Licences Drug Misuse Act makes this fairly easy to achieve. Again officially people, whoever they are, must be dealt with by the law and the courts and supplying Class A drugs is a very serious imprisonable offence with potentially even a life sentence.

We do see symbolic, local clampdowns on clubland but quite clearly there is no prospect of such a strategy becoming nationwide. It is unresourcable, unrealistic and anyway holds too many unintended consequences. The clubbers may not be wholly unstoppable but they would most certainly continue their alcohol and drug use if displaced by nightclub closure by relocating in the plethora of café bars now being routinely given alcohol and music/dancing licenses until 0200–0400 hours and awaiting further deregulation. Indeed, the extension of dance drug use, probably amphetamine and cocaine led, into this newly establishing time out sector, seems likely anyway.

In practice the state already operates a noninterventionist approach. It is never publicly announced, never written down but it is there at the local level. Leave the clubs and clubbers, beyond routine inspection, alone unless their behaviour attracts attention and makes an operational response a political necessity, or a pre-election vote winning soundbite can be harvested from symbolic persecution.

The practical consequences of this is that middle-class professional 'rising' and employed groups can use Class A drugs and take their chance with routine policing netting them but otherwise they will be left alone. Poor, unemployed Class A drug users will be urine tested, assessed and monitored via arrest referral schemes and criminal justice and prison interventions because they cannot afford to pay their drugs bills. We will store this contradiction as a further example of institutional dishonesty to be reviewed in Chapter 8.

6
Unreachable? The New Young Heroin Users

Howard Parker, Roy Egginton and Nicola Elson

Purpose

The problems the clubbers, at the serious end of recreational drug use, described were real enough. However, while we cannot be sure about the long-term health consequences of regular dance drug use their presenting problems with use appear largely manageable via self regulation. Most 'problem' drug use in the UK is associated with heroin and crack cocaine and was initially created with any density during the 1980s, through the first heroin cycle (described in Chapter 1). In this and Chapter 7 we provide regional case studies, utilizing qualitative techniques, describing how today's new poly drug problem users are emerging in 'hidden' worlds.

There are worrying signs that a new heroin cycle of local outbreaks is underway, but located within youth populations in small cities and regional towns rather than the inner areas and outer estates of the large city connurbations. An 'early warning' audit of new heroin spread is summarized leading on to a study profiling these new young heroin users.

The story of their deteriorating drugs careers and enveloping drugs–crime lifestyles is distressing, not just because many had conventional childhoods, but because their ill-conceived drugs careers have pulled them into the social exclusion zones. We find that throughout their adolescence today's new young dependent drug users remain hidden in their local community, largely unreached by official interventions.

In describing these evolving drugs careers we identify missed opportunities and lack of early interventions at home, at school, via local young people's and community services, family doctors and most importantly central government – the state. This does not bode well for the drugs strategy or the future of UK Drugs.

Introduction

In this chapter we illustrate how important exploratory 'early warning' research is, or more accurately should be, in developing a dynamic, strategic approach to better managing UK drugs. Given the dire consequences of the first heroin cycle and its legacy, one might expect government to be carefully monitoring the heavy end drugs scenes and sites, the underbelly of UK Drugs, to inform strategic and preventative measures. Not so. We summarize here two of only a handful of *ad hoc* studies undertaken at the end of the 1990s which attempt to describe evolving problematic drugs arenas. The first was an early warning audit exploring the possibility that heroin use was becoming more prevalent among the youth population, which we summarize briefly in the next section. The main thrust of this chapter is to describe how a small minority of young Britons are becoming involved with heroin and the impact heroin use has on their lives and, in time, the impact they have, as dependent users on others, be they friends, family or local community. This is attempted through qualitative interviews around England with 86 young people (14–21 years). They are largely 'hidden' heroin users who as 'recreational' drug triers in early adolescence were introduced to heroin via new availability in small cities and regional towns (with no previous heroin history). Their drugs journeys across adolescence illustrate both how 'unprotected' these young people were from the seductiveness of heroin but also how, once established, heavy end drugs careers can create numerous secondary problems which distance the now untrustworthy 'smackhead' from family and community.

We begin by summarizing the 'macro' national audit of new heroin outbreaks.

Attempting to Monitor New Heroin Spread

The heroin outbreaks of the 1980s 'settled' in the early 1990s with epidemic spread finally losing its energy. By then north west England, London, the Scottish cities and a clutch of Welsh communities in particular were learning to live with the consequences of hosting local heroin populations. Clearly in the endemic period of the early 1990s new heroin users did emerge including second generation users in the old sites, but in general heroin became relegated in the consciousness and concerns of government and indeed most young people. Drugs talk was dominated by the recreational scenes we have already described. However, signs of heroin uptake began to emerge during the mid 1990s as a number of small cities (for example Bradford, Bristol, Hull) and regional towns with no heroin history began to see an emergent heroin problem. In the absence of any monitoring system beyond seizures, treatment presentation and 'intelligence', government was persuaded to fund the audit we describe here.

A national postal survey of all Police Services and Drug Action Teams (DATs) was undertaken with extensive follow up telephone interviews all around the country and fieldwork visits in several areas claiming to be hosting new outbreaks or heroin 'hotspots' (Parker *et al.*, 1998a). The survey was aimed at key informants nominated by Chief Police Officers and DAT co-ordinators and they were asked to provide evidence of any new clusters of young heroin users emerging in their communities. The returns were patchy and, while at best we received 'presentation' data, seizure and arrest statistics, mortality rates and even summary of local in house research, for many areas we received more intuitive material and thus perceptions of say a local drugs agency manager or Police Drugs Squad inspector. Eventually 73 per cent of the DATs and 86 per cent of Police Forces made returns. This provided outline information for about 90 per cent of the two countries.

The picture to emerge from these local professionals and informants was unequivocal in respect of the geographical spread of new heroin outbreaks affecting young people. Overall 81 per cent of the Police Services and 80 per cent of the DATs making returns reported recent new clusters of heroin users within their jurisdictions. Many of these clusters were very small and only briefly described, whereas, quite significant outbreaks were reported by other areas. The non-returners were, in retrospect, highly likely to have no new outbreaks to report.

The picture to emerge was of a new geographical spread but in areas with *no* appreciable heroin history (eastern side of England, much of Yorkshire, south west England, parts of the Midlands). The old heroin areas reported little new incidence. It also emerged that a handful of small cities had been witnessing significant new outbreaks since 1993–94 with local officials only becoming professionally aware of this in retrospect. These particular cities appeared to have a heroin 'footprint' from the end of the first cycle (for example, older users in residence and established drug dealing systems).

A particularly worrying feature to emerge from Police evidence was that heroin was being purposefully marketed in towns on their patch having been transported from the wholesale warehouses in the old heroin cities, notably London and Liverpool, to these new markets. The motorways and the mobile phone have transformed the nature of macrodiffusion seen in earlier times (Hunt and Chambers, 1976), whereby, geographical distance is no longer a barrier to heroin spread. The increases in availability of heroin in the northern towns where we were monitoring adolescent drug trying (see Chapter 3) provided simultaneous evidence of this process.

Finally, although anecdotal, there was a strong sense in the survey returns that heroin uptake was prevalent beyond the vulnerable groups and the most deprived neighbourhoods of each town/city. Many return-ers raised concerns about its spread into the more mainstream youth population. Although we now go on to describe a follow up to this audit in respect of profiling these new young heroin users it is import-ant to note that no official attempts to further assess the validity of the audit's tentative conclusions were forthcoming. This in turn produces confusion and dispute which undermines clarity of purpose. For those in the outbreak regions the audit's conclusions remain accurate and robust but are viewed more sceptically by those, say in London, where cocaine rather than heroin is on the agenda. The epidemiology which easily explains how heroin and cocaine cycles and eras interrelate, which we discuss in the final chapter, is ignored. Complexity is unwelcome in the drugs discourse.

Accessing 'Hidden' Young Heroin Users

Following on from the national survey with its 'early warning' aspirations a small qualitative study was commissioned to provided a more sophis-ticated profile of the new young 'regional' heroin users. To further aid forecasting it was decided to try and locate adolescents relatively new to heroin, rather than interview twentysomethings via Community Drug Teams and methadone services. However it was also important to sample from several different regional sites.

In Chapter 7 we discuss how the use of indigenous fieldworkers is a particularly effective way of reaching hidden subterranean drugs worlds. In this study we had neither the time nor resources to set up such processes in four different areas and we thus fell back on a range of approaches. In Site One we relied on basing ourselves at a young person's drugs service and using posters and flyers to encourage both service users and their acquaintances/partners to be interviewed. A CD/music token was offered as an incentive throughout the study. As Table 6.1 shows this was not an altogether successful strategy. Despite the town experiencing a substantive heroin outbreak from 1995–96 and with over 1000 presenters at the local adult drugs service and needle exchange the younger newer users remained largely hidden.

Table 6.1   Outline of fieldwork

Fieldwork area	Interviews completed	Capture approach	Age of interviewees (mean)
Site One Town, northern England, east side (overall pop. 200 000)	12	Young person's drug service	18.7 years
Site Two Town, northern England, west side (overall pop. 270 000)	25	(4) Young persons drop-in (1) Community Drug Team (2) Youth Justice Team (18) Outreach on an estate	17.4 years
Site Three City, southern England, west side (overall pop. 350 000)	39	(3) Neighbourhood Community Project (15) Outreach (21) Young Person's Services networking	19.3 years
Site Four Small town, southern England, west side (overall pop. 30 000)	10	Outreach	18.6 years
	86		

In Site Two we extended our range of capture techniques and in particular set up our own sessional outreach centre in the coffee bar of a church hall and, with the help of a local person trusted by young drug users, 18 interviews were completed in five afternoon sessions on one housing estate. In Site Three we repeated the multiple approach and employed and trained up several experienced social work–community work professionals both to network out of a dedicated young person's service and through their community contacts. In Site Four we relied on one experienced outreach worker. The interviewers used a semi-structured schedule and the interviews themselves took at least one hour. A small self-complete questionnaire was also filled in by interviewees providing a summary of their drugs careers.

In retrospect we initially underestimated how 'insecure' and suspicious these young heroin users were of being interviewed. We had, through trial and error, to create a range of capture techniques in order to obtain interviews. Nearly all of these went well and, as we shall see, the reasons for this 'insecurity' became apparent from the interview material.

Demographic Characteristics of the Young Heroin Users

Overall 3.5 per cent of the sample were in the age group 14–15 years old. Both the 16–17 and the 18–19 age groups were represented by over a quarter of those interviewed. The remaining and largest concentration was found among those aged 20–21 years, making up 44.2 per cent of the sample. Approximately one in five (19.8 per cent) interviewees were female compared to 80.2 per cent males. In Sites One, Two and Three females were similarly outnumbered by their male counterparts, although parity between the sexes was achieved in Site Four. In terms of ethnic background 98.8 per cent (n = 85) identified themselves as 'white British' while 1.2 per cent (n = 1) indicated being Asian. The virtual absence of respondents from other ethnic groups renders any such comparison redundant. This does not mean ethnic minorities are not involved (Pearson and Patel, 1998).

The Social Exclusion 'At Risk' Measures

The impact of New Labour's emphasis on the social exclusion agenda has for drugs interventions been to highlight the correlation of heroin and crack cocaine use with social exclusion and vulnerability (*Drugs*, 1998; HAS, 1996; SSI, 1997). There is little doubt this linkage is very real (ACMD, 1998), but the development of recreational drug use during the 1990s and the wider availability of harder drugs right across the UK may well mean that more conventional, less impoverished young people may also take and become seduced by heroin, as is currently occurring in the USA (Jacobs, 1999). Both the Northern Regions Longitudinal Study (see Chapter 3) and the audit suggested this to be the case in England. In this study we thus carefully scrutinised the childhoods and family backgrounds of our sample of young heroin users to assess the nature and level of underlying 'exclusion' factors.

Childhood and family background

Over one-third of the respondents experienced 'highly disruptive' episodes during their upbringing. Only one in seven could be considered as having no 'disruption' during childhood.

> Dad left when I was five years old, I have hardly ever seen him. I'm glad because he used to beat up my mum. (Male, smoker three years, Site Three, 312).

> I was normal 'til then [parents split up], then it all went pear shaped. (Male, smoker–injector three years, Site One, 108)

While approximately four-fifths of these heroin users indicated that they had never had any 'in-care' experiences, half of the remainder (10.5 per cent) are considered as having had a 'high' degree of contact with social services based on their accounts.

In relation to income levels and quality of life indicators the socio-economic circumstances in which our sample grew up were relatively mixed. Over one-quarter (25.6 per cent) came from families with a 'high' reliance on state benefits, compared with almost 40 per cent who indicted no reliance on state welfare among parents and siblings. At the same time 12.8 per cent could be described as having a 'very poor' upbringing regarding issues centred on quality of life, involving the family's provision of new clothing, car ownership and frequency of family holidays. Finally, approximately half of the interviewees recollected or acknowledged some degree of alcohol or drug problems within their families as they were growing up.

> My mum's brother is a flat out drug user who injects whizz and heroin, he's been in a bad way for years. I first started smoking bongs with him when I was 11. (Male, smoker three years, Site Three, 312)

Overall these are not records of ideal childhoods as there are significant levels of disruption, family difficulties and relative poverty. On the other hand, most of the sample had not had highly problematic childhoods and certainly not to the extent that they all fit the classic vulnerable, excluded picture.

Discipline and parental supervision during adolescence

A key feature of adolescent 'risk taking' is being out with the peer group rather than home centred. All but one of the sample stated that, from around 13, they were often out with friends during days or evenings, over three-quarters indicated doing so every day/night. It was during many of these unsupervised periods that interviewees stated that they were experimenting with alcohol and drugs. Only 20.9 per cent stated that their parents/guardians knew where they were and what they were doing when they were out. This compares to 37.2 per cent whose parents knew where they were but *not* what they were doing and 40.7 per cent whose parents knew nothing of their whereabouts nor of what they were up to. Furthermore, three-quarters of the young people in this study stated that they lied to their parents about what they were doing when out of the family home. The cumulative effect of parents not knowing what their children were doing inevitably exacerbated confrontations in some households. Such confrontations were often given as the reason why many (60 per cent) of the interviewees ran away or 'stayed out' all night.

> Mum couldn't really handle me at home, I was starting to get in trouble with the police and at school. Me step-dad was always going on about the effect on his kids. We still don't get on, he can't stand me. (Male, smoker two years, Site Two, 223)

> I try not to stay at mum's cos of me step-dad, it's better for her that I don't stick around too much, it just leads to arguments. (Male, smoker two years, Site Two, 223)

> Any place they put me in, I always got out, I could escape from anywhere. (Female, injector five years plus, Site Two, 206)

Schooling and qualifications

Although 4.7 per cent of the young heroin users we interviewed stated that they were still of school age none of them actually attended. Disaffection regarding school life was felt to varying degrees by around three-quarters of the sample, 39.5 per cent stated they 'disliked school' and 33.7 per cent had 'mixed' feelings about their school days leaving only 24.4 per cent who indicated they 'liked school'. While opinions of school were relatively mixed, truancy was almost universal with 94 per cent of respondents indicating truancy episodes. Although the frequency with which our interviewees truanted varied greatly there was extensive school absence.

In terms of schoolwork and qualification results the interviews show a fairly mixed picture. When asked how they rated their schoolwork in comparison to that of their contemporaries 42.9 per cent believed that their work was worse, 36.9 per cent felt it to be of the same standard, and 19 per cent indicated that it was better. Overall, 48.2 per cent of the sample stated that they had no academic qualifications. The rest of the sample was relatively well qualified. Approximately 56 per cent of those with qualifications had from 1 to 11 GCSEs under grade C while 44 per cent indicated having 1 to 11 GCSEs graded at C or above. Almost one third of those with qualifications also had NVQs while just under 5 per cent indicated that they had 'A' levels.

Disillusionment with school was matched and calibrated by considerable levels of enforced exclusion, with 63.9 per cent experiencing temporary exclusions and 43.5 per cent indicating that they had been permanently excluded at least once during their secondary school careers. The five most common reasons for official exclusions cited were 'general misbehaviour' (57.6 per cent), 'fighting' (42.4 per cent), 'drinking alcohol/smoking' (16.9 per cent) 'truancy' (16.9 per cent) and 'violence towards teachers or other pupils' (15.3 per cent). The 'taking and/or selling of drugs in school' was the sixth most common reason cited by 13.6 per cent of excludees.

Smoking Tobacco, Drinking Alcohol and Trying and Use of Illicit Drugs

Smoking and drinking

Smoking cigarettes and/or tobacco was almost universal within this sample with 97.7 per cent indicating that they were current smokers. All of these respondents also indicated that they smoked 'every day'. The average age for trying cigarettes or tobacco for the first time was 11.89 years old. In Site Four the mean age for first time cigarette trying was over three years younger than that found in Site One (10.90 years compared to 13.92 years). Overall, the average number of cigarettes smoked by young people in the seven days prior to the interview was 114.

The mean age of first trying an alcoholic drink was recalled as 12.72 years old. It was clear from their histories that nearly all the sample were early drinkers and that smoking and drinking were their initial 'psycho-active' experiences, particularly when hanging out with friends in early adolescence. We failed to quantify this picture accurately during the interview focusing instead on current drinking patterns. Many heavy end drug users give up and become only occasional users of alcohol and it is not surprising therefore that while 59.3 per cent were still 'current' drinkers only 7.2 per cent drank every day, 14.5 per cent two or three times and 16.9 per cent only once in the week preceding the interview. However these weekly drinkers did have big appetites consuming a mean of 43.3 units of alcohol.

Illicit drugs trying and use

Table 6.2 summarizes the drugs histories of our sample. Their mean age of heroin initiation was 15.4 years. This is important, because prior to

Table 6.2 Drugs tried, last time used and mean age when first tried for young heroin users

Last time used drug column percentage (n = 86)	Tried (%)	Never tried (%)	Over a year ago (%)	In past year (%)	In past 6 months (%)	In the past month (%)	Mean age first tried (yrs)
Amphetamines	91.8	8.2	43.5	20.0	21.2	7.1	14.79
Nitrites	76.7	23.3	62.8	9.3	3.5	1.2	14.15
Cannabis	98.8	1.2	9.6	1.2	7.2	80.6	12.67
Cocaine	55.3	44.7	28.0	10.5	15.3	9.4	16.64
Crack	75.3	24.7	10.6	11.8	20.0	33.0	16.71
LSD	83.5	16.5	65.9	7.1	5.9	4.8	14.29
Magic mushrooms	57.6	42.4	50.6	4.7	1.2	1.2	14.30
Ecstasy	64.3	35.7	39.3	13.1	9.5	2.4	15.92
Solvents/gas	65.5	34.5	57.1	3.5	1.2	3.6	12.90
Anabolic steroids	2.3	97.7	1.2	0.0	1.2	0.0	13.00
Tranquillisers	82.1	17.9	14.3	9.5	13.1	45.2	16.00
Methadone	81.0	19.0	13.1	11.9	10.7	45.2	16.94
Other illegal drugs*	8.4	91.6	4.8	1.2	1.2	1.2	16.71

* denotes only other 'illegal' drug tried/used was Ketamine.

this we can see that the order of initiation follows that typically found in the 'recreational' using population, with cannabis having the earliest onset (12.67 years) followed by solvents/gases (12.9), nitrites (14.15), LSD (14.29), magic mushrooms (14.3) and amphetamines (14.79). With ecstasy trying at age 15–16 we should also note that the other more 'serious' drugs of tranquillisers (16.0), cocaine (16.64), crack cocaine (16.71) and methadone just before age 17 all follow heroin initiation. As we shall see this is a consequence of these young heroin users taking up these secondary drugs and gradually becoming poly drug users.

The rates of early onset drug trying and use in the sample far outstrip those found in the Northern Regions Longitudinal Study described in Chapter 3. Even the clubbers, the most serious recreational users, have more modest antecedents.

Damaged Childhoods and Adolescence?

The childhoods of this sample were far from ideal. Most experienced some family disruption. Over half lived in families where there was some reliance on state benefits. On the other hand less than 20 per cent had experienced 'care' episodes and half had families with one or both parents in employment. The picture is thus complex, the classic 'at risk' factors are present but far from all embracing certainly when compared with studies of 'vulnerable' groups and problem drug uses which receive most attention (for example, care leavers, homeless young people).

Where things go more overtly wrong is in early adolescence. Two-thirds of the sample acknowledged discipline problems at home and a similar proportion were involved in school exclusions. Their educational qualifications although again diverse, generally beg the label 'underqualified'. These problems are symptomatic of risk taking street-wise pathways through adolescence illustrated by early onset of tobacco and alcohol use and very early florid drug trying mimicking the order of initiation found among 1990s adolescence but without the cost–benefit boundaries employed by most young drug triers.

A reasonable conclusion is that while the risk criteria of social exclusion are important they are not definitive. The childhoods and family life of our subjects are best seen as towards the 'at risk' end on a series of dimensions but also embracing those with tolerable, unremarkable backgrounds we find among a significant minority of contemporary youth. This suggests that in these English regions with new outbreaks, susceptibility to heroin trying must be viewed as embracing a slightly wider population than the classically 'socially excluded'.

Heroin Careers: Initiation, Evolution and Current Use Status

In this section we look specifically at the heroin–poly drug careers of the sample. Remarkably the age of initiation for heroin was at age 15 in each site. This is over two years younger than onset found during the 1980s heroin outbreaks (Parker *et al.*, 1988).

Initiation

The most common initiating location was a 'friend's home' cite by nearly 40 per cent of respondents, followed by 'outside' (9.1 per cent), 'at home' (7.6 per cent), school (3 per cent) and youth centre (3 per cent). Over three-quarters of heroin initiations took place in the company of friends who were contemporaries at the time with almost one-third stating that older friends were present. Only 3.6 per cent (two male interviewees) said that they were alone when they first tried heroin and six per cent (mainly female respondents) indicated that they were with their then partners. Interestingly in Sites Three and Four, 13.9 per cent and 40 per cent of respondents respectively stated that their initiations involved sprinkling heroin over cannabis and/or tobacco mounted on a 'bong' or in a pipe and smoking it.

> We all had a try on the bong, we were already smoking dope on it and just put a sprinkle [of heroin] on top. It felt pretty nice, a warm feeling. (Male, smoker five years or more, Site Four, 308)

Heroin initiation usually involved a small dose and in general this was not only tempered by cautious curiosity, but also by the fact that those helping the initiate would often be heroin users themselves and thus unwilling to share too much of their own supply. However, even the effects of a few lines of heroin on the first occasion can often render any desire to immediately repeat the dose impractical, as over one-third of initiations end in vomiting. Although adverse responses to first time trying account for over 40 per cent of respondents' recollections of the event, over half stated that their first heroin experience was 'good'.

The most common method employed for taking or administering heroin was smoking (or chasing) and was cited by 90.7 per cent of initiates. Injecting on these first occasions was experienced by only 3.5 per cent of interviewees. Of those who stated whether or not they were 'helped' by others during initiation 26.5 per cent said that 'friends' helped them 'run the lines'. Eight in ten (79.3 per cent) of interviewees tried heroin again at some point within a month of initiation. Given that over half of the sample had defined their initiation as a 'good' experience and with the rest not being deterred by adverse experiences – some even enjoyed being sick – it is not surprising that heroin careers develop quickly. Therefore, in general, for this sample more regular and frequent use soon followed the initiation period as users moved from occasional to weekly and eventually daily use.

Another feature of these developing heroin careers is the progression from smoking to trying injection. While only 3.5 per cent of interviewees recalled injecting as the method used during initiation, by the time we conducted our interviews over two-thirds (67.4 per cent) of respondents indicated that they had tried injecting heroin. The largest concentration of those who said that they had 'ever injected' were found among respondents in Sites One and Three (75 per cent and 87.2 per cent respectively), almost double that found in the other two field-work sites. Young men were significantly more likely to have tried injecting than the young women in the study (72.5 per cent compared to 47.1 per cent). As with smoking/chasing heroin those who chose to try injecting often needed help from more experienced users in order to perform the procedure correctly and safely. Half of those who had tried injecting imparted information about whether the needle had been used prior to their injecting initiation. Of these respondents nine out of ten stated that they knew the needle was clean, with the remainder knowing that someone else had used the needle previously.

Contemplating 'giving up' is already prevalent among these heroin users. Nearly 70 per cent of respondents (excluding those who currently are not using heroin) in our sample had attempted 'self-detox'. Many of these respondents stated that they had tried self-detoxing on several occasions, however, because respondents could not easily quantify these events it is difficult to clarify this information. Respondents who attempted the self-detox were often 'helped' by parents, partners or even siblings who would prevent them from leaving the house some-times for up to three weeks. Often, though, such events would end in failure with the respondent reverting back to heroin use, in some cases within a matter of a few days. These repeated attempts, while they illus-trate how out of control many respondents felt their heroin use was, need to be harnessed in official intervention, not least because they are related to subsequent overdosing and deaths found in this population.

Current heroin use status

Table 6.3 is a composite table that not only shows the current use status of our sample but also summarizes the current methods of administration used, typical quantities of heroin consumed and length of use. As we can see although the length of time a respondent has been using heroin appears to be evenly distributed overall it does vary from site to site. This is primarily a product of our recruitment strategies and the different sites being at distinctive stages of their outbreaks.

The method of 'only smoking' heroin was more prevalent in Sites Two and Four, accounting for around two-thirds of users in each area. Injecting only was significantly higher among respondents in Site Three (43.6 per cent) than in any other site but we must remember these interviewees were older and had longer drugs careers. However, injecting was also prevalent in Site One with half of respondents indicating that they used 'both' methods.

Table 6.3 also depicts the current use status of our sample in terms of regularity and frequency of use. Almost two-thirds (65.1 per cent) of the interviewees were 'daily' users and were relatively evenly spread throughout the fieldwork sites. The amount of heroin used by our respondents although seemingly high does vary between sites, age group and according to regularity and administration method. Overall daily users imbibed higher quantities than those using on a less regular basis. Also, higher quantities were used by daily users in Site Three than daily users in the other three sites. In general the older and more experienced the respondent the more heroin they used on a weekly basis, for instance 20–21 year olds used 2.76 grams per week compared to 14–15 year olds who used 1.40 grams per week. Finally, in respect to weekly use rates according to the current method of use, injectors used on average twice as much heroin as smokers (3.37 compared to 1.66 grams).

Those respondents who said that they had stopped using heroin at the time of the interview represent almost one-sixth (15.1 per cent) of our sample and as previously mentioned were evenly spread across the fieldwork sites. However, these respondents reported heavy past use of heroin and are indeed the highest recorded in this study with an overall weekly average of 3.66 grams (equivalent to more than five bags per day). These respondents had, on average, stopped using heroin for approximately three and a half months.

The Consequences and Costs of Heroin Dependency

Introduction

In this section we focus on the costs and consequences of growing heroin dependency. Clearly our subjects were at different stages of their classic heroin career. Some at age 16–17 (in Site Two) were novice smokers

Table 6.3 Current use status among young heroin users

		Site One	Site Two	Site Three	Site Four	All
n size		12	25	39	10	86
Column percentage		%	%	%	%	%
Current heroin use status	daily users	75.0	60.0	66.7	60.0	65.1
	2–3 times p/wk users	0.0	24.0	10.3	10.0	12.8
	occasional users	0.0	0.0	12.8	10.0	7.0
	given up	25.0	16.0	10.3	20.0	15.1
Current method of administration	only smokes	8.3	68.0	20.5	60.0	37.2
	only injects	16.7	12.0	43.6	0.0	25.6
	both	50.0	0.0	25.6	20.0	20.9
	other	0.0	4.0	0.0	0.0	1.2
	given up	25.0	16.0	10.3	20.0	15.1
Length of use (yrs)	One year	16.7	56.0	2.6	10.0	20.9
	Two years	25.0	24.0	12.8	10.0	17.4
	Three years	41.7	8.0	25.6	40.0	24.4
	Four years	16.7	8.0	20.5	10.0	15.1
	Five years or more	0.0	1.0	38.5	30.0	22.1
Mean grams of heroin used per week by current use status	daily users	1.44	2.29	3.08	2.39	2.53
	2–3 times p/wk users	–	0.28	0.55	0.35	0.38
	occasional users	–	–	0.49	0.02	0.39
	stoppers (given up)	2.57	3.27	5.95	3.50	3.66

Mean grams of heroin used per week according to current method of administration	only smokes	2.28	1.55	1.48	1.99	1.66
	only injects	0.88	4.03	3.58	–	3.37
	both	1.33	–	1.31	1.40	1.32
	other	–	0.02	–	–	0.02
Mean number of years since user started taking heroin more than once per week	daily users	1.92	1.96	3.66	2.40	2.77
	2–3 times p/wk users	–	1.52	2.63	–	2.01
	occasional users	–	–	3.20	1.17	2.86
	stoppers (given up)	2.00	1.04	3.88	2.75	2.40
Mean number of months since those who have 'given up' last used heroin		2.8	3.3	5.0	2.9	3.6

whereas in Site Three we found 18–20 year olds immersed deep in the problems of injecting and using crack cocaine alongside their brown and methadone. Nevertheless, there are patterns in their profiles and we find remarkable symmetry given the geographical distinctiveness of each site across England.

We must return to the social exclusion debate but this time arguing that even if many of our subjects began their adolescence in tolerably supportive arrangements their heroin careers ensured their social realignment was towards the margins. We locate this with growing heroin dependency, poly drug use and subsequent problems with personal health, expulsions, drugs bills, and an increasing reliance on acquisitive crime and drug dealing to supplement legitimate income, mainly derived from state benefits.

Exclusion, realignment and stigma

As previously noted, our sample found their integration, performance and indeed access to school increasingly undermined as a result of their erratic attendance and problematic behaviour, which coincided with mid 1990s stringent school exclusion policies (SCODA, 1999). In parallel their insistence on being 'out and about' all the time, engaging in a florid drinking and drug trying period and initiating on heroin at around age 15 was also incubating a break with more normative, conventional friends. This friction was with school and neighbourhood friends who would, for instance, only smoke cannabis and regarded heroin trying as beyond the pale.

> Some lads I used to smoke draw with think I'm mad for startin' on heroin. (Male, smoker two years, Site Two, 208)

Many of our interviewees had also been early clubbers but again heroin had separated them from the dance drug users they socialised with.

> I was single at the time, work was getting me down, nothing in life seemed to be going right. It was just escapism, something I looked forward to. It was a social thing in the beginning, clubbing was getting boring and I made a new group of friends through using [heroin]. (Female, smoker three years, Site Three, 310)

This process went further with heroin trying networks also suffering attrition as some triers stepped back and avoided further contact with heroin in the only way they could – by absenting themselves from the network. There were suggestions that the smoking only or injecting axis produced further peer realignment. This same process affected many family relationships triggering feelings of loss and breakdown. Over 60 per cent of the sample had left home at the time of interview.

> Heroin has made me angry, I would go and hit my mum because of drug use. I was thrown out of home because of heroin. (Male, smoker–injector five years, Site Three, 336)
>
> I've been living with my granma for six months after mum and dad kicked me out for stealin' for heroin and cannabis. (Male, smoker one year, Site Two, 216)
>
> Heroin has affected me relationship with me mum, pulled us apart. (Male injector five years, Site Three, 304)
>
> Started stealing from work to pay for it [heroin]. I lost my job because I was caught stealing. Mum and Dad had enough and I got kicked out. I moved into a friend's house and we started selling heroin. (Male, smoker four years, Site Three, 338)

These on-going fractures and tensions with straighter friends and family, plus the failure to attempt or succeed at gaining/sustaining employment, are brought together by the status of becoming an outsider and being labelled or defined as a *baghead*, *pinhead* or *smackhead* (Finnigan, 1996).

> At a family party recently I was speaking to a girl I know and her boyfriend called her over and told her not to speak to us because we were smackheads. . . . I felt really hurt and we left in case the family overheard what was being said. (Female, smoker three years, Site Four, 310)

Such labelling involves being attributed motives and behaviours that can over predict actual deviant behaviour and produce a sense of injustice.

> My heroin use affected everything in a big way. I didn't steal from my parents and never used in the house . . . I was still chucked out simply because I use gear. (Male, smoker five years, Site Three, 317)

Patently all these processes become intertwined and some are more potent than others for each subject and through time. Those acknowledging their dependency or addiction and contemplating giving up were often able to take a wider view, perhaps encouraged by advice or counselling.

> Heroin has ruined every relationship I've had. All the girlfriends I've had I've lost because of drugs, mother, father, brother lost through drugs. There's no trust with friends. (Male, injector four years, Site Three, 327)

Through these processes regular users find themselves associating increasingly with other heroin users, some of whom are friends, others merely fellow travellers who, to an extent, look out for each other. The strong propensity in this age group is for heroin using men and women to co-habit or indeed for one user, usually the male, to initiate and facilitate the use of heroin by their partners. These couplings are often functional while both wish to carry on using heroin.

> He [partner] uses so he understands especially because he's been on it ages longer than me. (Female, smoker two years, Site Four, 318)

Indeed this heroin routine may not easily be disturbed by methadone.

> I'd prefer either gear or meth' but my boyfriend's 'earning' all day and by the time he's come back with the gear I've been clucking and had my meth', so I end up having both. (Female, smoker two years, Site Four, 318)

Despite these arrangements, four in ten of the sample still lived with parents or in the family home. However, whether living at home or not, or on good terms with parents or not, 73 per cent of this sample still saw 'mum' as the most significant person in their lives; a far higher rating even than romantic partners and, therefore, a potentially important agent for reintegration. The fact that these new young heroin users are *not* predominantly from dysfunctional families, nor have grown up in care, means the family bond may possibly be a vehicle for positive change and intervention (Newburn and Elliot, 1999) as some individuals contemplate giving up heroin and/or crack cocaine, and their consequent downward spiral (Elland-Goossensen *et al.*, 1998).

For some, however, support structures of most importance remain inadequate and even bizarre.

> My friend whose me dealer. He's been me dealer since I was nine or ten...I feel like he's always there for me. He even came to visit me when I was in prison. I tried to give up heroin a few months back and he was trying to help me thru' me rattle, I only lasted eight hours. (Female, injector five years, Site Two, 206)

Table 6.4 Self reported health problems arising from heroin use

	Site One	Site Two	Site Three	Site Four	All
n size	12	25	39	10	86
Column percentage	%	%	%	%	%
Indicated health had been affected by drug/heroin use	83.3	60.0	77.8	75.0	72.8
General health (e.g. fitness, lethargy, illness prone)	40.0	66.7	64.3	83.3	62.7
Eating disorders/weight loss	40.0	26.7	35.7	50.0	35.6
Respiratory problems	20.0	33.3	39.3	16.7	32.2
Blood/skin disorders	30.0	6.7	35.7	32.3	27.1
Psycho-emotional problems	20.0	0.0	10.7	16.7	10.2
Intestinal/stomach disorders	20.0	0.0	3.6	16.7	6.8
Urinary/genito-urinary problems	0.0	0.0	10.7	0.0	5.1
Bones, joints (oesteo)	0.0	0.0	7.1	16.7	5.1
Dental	0.0	6.7	7.1	0.0	5.1
Personal hygiene	0.0	13.3	0.0	0.0	3.4
Menstrual	0.0	0.0	3.6	0.0	1.7
Other problems	0.0	0.0	3.6	0.0	1.7
Don't know	0.0	6.7	0.0	0.0	1.7

Problems with Personal Health

Table 6.4 shows the personal health problems that interviewees attribute to their heroin use: over seven-in-ten believe these health disorders to be a consequence of their drug use. There were no marked differences in morbidity by gender although the young men reported far more 'general health' problems, while females were often more specific, reporting more blood/skin disorders (36.4 per cent), more genito/urinary problems (18.2 per cent), bone/joint problems (18.2 per cent) and psycho-emotional problems (18.2 per cent).

Age and length of use also held interesting practical significance with our youngest, least heroin experienced users being just as likely to report 'general health' problems suggesting that they are already recognizing the 'price' of heroin early in their careers – again a potential lever for early intervention.

Growing heroin and poly drug dependency

Although individual users differ in respect to tolerance, routes of administration, intake levels and so on, the overall picture is not one of sudden addiction but of creeping dependency in which quite long periods of enjoyment, notably honeymooning and gouching, can be obtained. Heroin use also gives rise to other positive effects related to feeling safe, secure and carefree and because these 'benefits' are felt with the greatest intensity early in a career or when switching to injecting or combining other drugs, (notably tranquillisers and crack cocaine) the motivation to carry on is considerable.

> By the time I was seventeen I started using a bit of crack as well. Its almost like they are boyfriend and girlfriend. I use crack sometimes because I get bored with gear. (Male, smoker 5 years, Site Three, 317)
>
> It makes me feel safe, like I'm coming home. I always used to be cold . . . heroin makes me warm. . . . I was anorexic, I loved it because it made me sick. (Female, injector four years, Site Three, 334)
>
> It [crack] makes me appreciate heroin more. (Female, smoker two years, Site Three, 331)

However through time and regular use tolerance builds up and dependency sets in producing the classic problematic heroin or poly drug career. As Table 6.5 shows, the journey to dependency, regret, contemplation and giving up may take several years.

For each of the dependency criteria interviewees scored themselves on we find length of use and age correlate with increased dependency, as anxiety and disenchantment with a drugs lifestyle and its all-embracing effects grow. Those at the beginning of their careers do not experience their heroin use as being out of control. Most do not become anxious or worried about whether they can 'top up'. Over half remain agnostic about giving up and believe they could do so if they wanted. Through time most experience less control over their use and become increasingly focused on the next dose and safe supplies, anxiety levels rise and increasingly they contemplate stopping but simultaneously realise how difficult this is and how they would miss their drugs dreadfully.

In general the scores in Table 6.5 suggest we already have a dependent population making up the sample, a proportion of whom will have other psychological difficulties.

I wish I could stop it like that, but it's not that easy. It takes away everything negative, every negative thought or feeling, it's mental addiction. (Female, injector two years, Site One, 112)

I look back when I started using and think how good it was back then. I don't get off on it anymore. I just hurt less. I wish I could gouch again, but it never does. (Male, smoker five years, Site Three, 313)

I feel like shit. We don't want to be like this for the rest of our lives. We have to do it now just to feel normal. (Male, smoker five years, Site Four, 313)

With all the sample being heavy tobacco smokers, which in itself is likely to trigger morbidity, over 70 per cent cannabis users, one-quarter current users of tranquillisers (some on prescription) and one-third taking methadone, it is hard to isolate what this sample is dependent on. Of most concern is the fact that three-quarters have tried crack cocaine and one-quarter in the 'past week'.

Increasing involvement in crime

Although some academic debate rambles on in respect of the drugs–crime relationship the overall picture is fairly clear. There are several different types of relationship depending on the population, the drug and the context (Walters, 1994). The basic conclusions from an impressive research literature built up over the past 20 years in respect of heroin (and more recently crack cocaine) and young adults are widely accepted. The common sense notion that heroin use leads to crime is inadequate. This unidirectional relationship can be found in a minority of users where their conventional lifestyles are undermined by growing dependency and drugs bills. We are also likely to find this among more conventional users where theft from the home or work emerges as a direct consequence of drugs bills. More often British studies have found that delinquency often pre-dates heroin use, whereby, a whole series of rule breaking behaviours, including drug use and offending, run parallel through adolescence (Hough, 1996). Heroin dependency thus amplifies these criminal careers and focuses them on acquisitive offending, notably shoplifting, general theft, burglary and fraud (Parker and Newcombe, 1987). Drug dealing and prostitution are other 'deviant' routes commonly associated with problematic drug use (see Chapter 7). Although it was difficult to fully explore this with our sample due to the complexities of the issue, problems of recollection and so on, it was possible to gain some insights.

Table 6.5 Dependency and anxiety by length of heroin use

length of use		1 yr	2 yrs	3 yrs	4 yrs	5 yrs +	All
n size		18	15	21	13	19	86
Column percentage		(%)	(%)	(%)	(%)	(%)	(%)
Did you ever think that your heroin use was out of control?	never/almost never	50.0	13.3	10.0	30.8	11.1	21.3
	sometimes	21.4	40.0	35.0	23.1	38.9	32.5
	often	14.3	26.7	30.0	23.1	11.1	21.3
	always/nearly always	14.3	20.0	25.0	23.1	38.9	25.0
	mean score	1.93	2.53	2.70	2.38	2.78	2.50
Did the prospect of not taking heroin make you very anxious or worried?	never/almost never	46.7	13.3	5.0	30.8	5.6	18.5
	sometimes	13.3	26.7	25.0	7.7	27.8	21.0
	often	40.0	20.0	40.0	30.8	16.7	29.6
	always/nearly always	0.0	40.0	30.0	30.8	50.0	30.9
	mean score	1.93	2.87	2.95	2.62	3.11	2.73

Did you worry about	never/almost never	33.3	6.7	5.0	7.7	5.6	11.1
your heroin use?	sometimes	20.0	26.7	10.0	23.1	16.7	18.5
	often	13.3	20.0	50.0	23.1	27.8	28.4
	always/nearly always	33.3	46.7	35.0	46.2	50.0	42.0
	mean score	2.47	3.07	3.15	3.08	3.22	3.01
Did you wish you could	never/almost never	26.7	0.0	10.0	0.0	0.0	7.4
stop using heroin?	sometimes	20.0	6.7	5.0	7.7	5.6	8.6
	often	6.7	26.7	30.0	30.8	11.1	21.0
	always/nearly always	46.7	66.7	55.0	61.5	83.3	63.0
	mean score	3.73	3.60	3.30	3.54	3.78	3.40
How difficult would	easy	25.0	0.0	0.0	15.4	0.0	7.3
you find it to stop, or	quite	25.0	46.7	42.1	38.5	10.5	31.7
go without heroin?	very	37.5	40.0	52.6	38.5	52.6	45.1
	impossible	12.5	13.3	5.3	7.7	36.8	15.9
	mean score	2.37	2.67	2.63	2.38	3.26	2.70

Given their extensive drugs careers it is not surprising that six in ten (57 per cent) had a caution or conviction for possession or supply of drugs (mean 1.4 cautions or convictions), divided equally between Class A (for example heroin, ecstasy) and Class B (for example cannabis) drugs. Very few had a supply indictment with personal possession dominating their antecedents. There were few obvious gender or site differences but rates of conviction increased with age and length of use of heroin. The dominant mode of punishment was the caution, with fines, probation and community service and custody in particular being applied in only a small minority of cases.

Previous criminal offence cautions and convictions offer further insights, with 91 per cent of interviewees having received a caution or conviction (mean number of indictments was high at 10.8), suggesting a fairly criminogenic sample. In terms of levels and types of crime there were few differences by site and age although length of use predicted increased conviction. The majority of females (77 per cent) had indictments, but mostly cautions, primarily for shoplifting, although nearly four in ten had criminal cases pending at the time of interview. Among males the dominant processed offence was also shoplifting, far outstripping any other offences but followed by 'TWOCing' (car theft), assaults and violence, burglary, theft, robbery, vandalism and criminal damage. Although cautions were the usual sanction, most had been sentenced by a court with fines and community supervisions, while 14 per cent of young men had been in custody and 14 per cent had cases pending.

While this pattern of offending is primarily acquisitive, less instrumental offences such as assault are also prevalent. Such behaviour was spread across their adolescence, again suggesting some propensity to delinquency is present independent of heroin related offending (Kaye *et al.*, 1998).

Funding Expensive Habits

Table 6.6 documents typical illicit drugs expenditure reported for the seven days prior to each interview (or last seven days of typical use).

Table 6.6   Expenditure on heroin and other illicit drugs in the last seven days by Site

	Site One	*Site Two*	*Site Three*	*Site Four*	*All*
size	12	25	39	10	86
Mean £ on heroin	138.89	152.98	135.91	89.38	£136.09
Mean £ total drugs bill	173.30	179.39	163.79	95.20	£160.56

Overall 83 per cent of the sample felt their calculations were typical of their using patterns. These are fairly consistent expenditure patterns given the differences in locality and suggest a reasonably accurate estimate for these younger users. Annual expenditure is around £8000 and seems to fit well with bills of about £10 000 for more established twenty-something users. When we take out the 13 temporary or permanent stoppers and divide the current users into daily, two to three times a week and occasional users, we find that the daily user bills rise to £206 (all drugs), the weekly users spending £50 and more occasional users £81. We also find injectors have the highest drugs bills. Surprisingly length of use did not correlate with increased weekly bills.

Given that hardly any of the sample (about 6 per cent) were in employment it seems likely that state benefits, which 80 per cent were in receipt of, provides a key source of income (in Site One for instance benefit books were sometimes left with or confiscated by dealers as 'insurance'). The acquisitive crimes dedicated to funding drugs bills, although diverse, were dominated by shoplifting, while a significant minority of males were involved in drug dealing. Such deviant funding routes rarely show up in official crime statistics.

Reaching out and Early Interventions

Unreached young users

While 87 per cent of the sample said they were registered with a General Practitioner and almost two thirds of the sample indicated contact with their doctor regarding their heroin use, many described these interactions in negative terms. Aside from the longer term users' passing attendance at local needle exchanges we can see how only limited engagement has taken place. To this we must add that those street level community projects claiming to be working with young heroin users appeared to see far less than we would expect and were regarded with suspicion by our interviewees.

This returns us to the issues of (in)security, self confidence and trust. We can see how our youngest users have very little contact with any potential points of help. They also had a strong tendency to DNA – do not attend a service they had contemplated visiting. Along with waiting lists this fall in the age of onset of drug use seems likely to delay presentation.

All this, we believe, requires the drugs interventions industry to *reach out* to young heroin users. They are too insecure, ambivalent and 'unskilled' to present to services run by, as they see it, unsympathetic, unpredictable adults in authority. They have little concept of what a

Table 6.7   Contact with local services by length of heroin use

Length of use		1 yr	2 yrs	3 yrs	4 yrs	5 yrs +	All
n size		18	15	21	13	19	86
Column percentage		%	%	%	%	%	%
GP	current	11.1	26.7	42.9	30.8	63.2	36.0
	past service user	0.0	13.3	42.9	38.5	26.3	24.4
	DNA	27.8	6.7	0.0	0.0	0.0	7.0
	attended only once	5.6	6.7	4.8	0.0	5.3	4.7
Young person's (general) service	current	11.1	0.0	0.0	7.7	5.3	4.7
	past service user	0.0	0.0	0.0	0.0	0.0	0.0
	DNA	33.3	6.7	0.0	0.0	0.0	8.1
	attended only once	0.0	0.0	0.0	0.0	0.0	0.0
Young person's (drug) service	current	16.7	20.0	23.8	0.0	36.8	20.9
	past service user	5.6	0.0	14.3	0.0	5.3	5.8
	DNA	27.8	6.7	0.0	0.0	0.0	7.0
	attended only once	0.0	0.0	0.0	0.0	0.0	0.0
CDT/Drug clinic	current	5.6	6.7	14.3	15.4	10.5	10.5
	past service user	5.6	6.7	0.0	0.0	21.1	7.0
	DNA	27.8	6.7	0.0	0.0	0.0	7.0
	attended only once	0.0	0.0	0.0	0.0	0.0	0.0
Street Agency/ Drop-in	current	0.0	26.7	28.6	30.8	36.8	24.4
	past service user	11.1	6.7	23.8	7.7	26.3	16.3
	DNA	27.8	6.7	0.0	0.0	5.3	8.1
	attended only once	0.0	0.0	0.0	0.0	10.5	2.3
Needle exchange	current	5.6	40.0	19.0	38.5	42.1	27.9
	past service user	11.1	6.7	4.8	7.7	15.8	9.3
	DNA	27.8	0.0	0.0	0.0	0.0	5.8
	attended only once	0.0	0.0	0.0	7.7	5.3	2.3
Other	current	11.1	0.0	9.5	0.0	5.3	5.8
	past service user	0.0	6.7	9.5	7.7	5.3	5.8
	DNA	0.0	0.0	0.0	0.0	0.0	0.0
	attended only once	0.0	0.0	0.0	0.0	0.0	0.0

service is and what it might offer. Reaching out from a young person's service centre is likely to be more effective than traditional outreach. Given the poor track record of 'unaccountable' outreach workers, in our view, staff from a young person's service should both take elements of their service out to hidden users and also act as advocates to bring them in through trust building, rehearsals and a commitment to confidentiality. This approach also facilitates effective management of the workers in the field. The case for sensitising other local professionals in touch with young people about heroin careers through delivering more soph-isticated information and training is also recommended as it is a serious blockage to appropriate advice and referral (Newburn and Elliot, 1999). The new pastoral/mentoring workers being located in secondary schools must be a target for such awareness training.

It also seems vital to be able to simultaneously accommodate *groups* of service users. The heroin network offers support for the new service user and the opportunity to work with it to influence each and every member. Similarly couples need to be accommodated. While this approach is fairly familiar to youth workers it is alien to many drugs services. The referral, waiting list and appointment procedures currently employed make such group work problematic.

Early intervention opportunities

We have had to refer repeatedly to the lack of accurate information and advice our young heroin users have received about heroin and poly drug use and to their overall naivety about the consequences of using heroin. Their main sources of information are personal experience and talking with or observing fellow users and dealers. While secondary pre-vention/harm reduction strategies have been undertaken with older users we have almost no experience of reaching out to such a young 'hidden' group who are clearly (in)articulating their relative ignorance.

> If I would have known what it does or what would happen. If I'd known it was heroin. I was told it was like powdered cannabis. (Male, smoker five years, Site Three, 313)
>
> Can you get AIDs from taking heroin? (Male, smoker one year, Site Two, informal)
>
> Other people set their limits but I always wanted to try everything and did. Wasn't warned about if it was harmful. I didn't know about addiction and shit like that, I just knew the good points. (Male, injector five years, Site Three, 339)

Clearly a whole range of initiatives could be developed for these young heroin users. We offer two examples. First, we have noted that over 70 per cent of the sample indicated that they had attempted to 'detox'. Most failed and we also know that overdosing and deaths are associated with redosing after such periods. Targeted public health mes-sages need to reach this group who need to know how to harness their contemplation to change, how to avoid overdosing and how to help those who do (Strang *et al.*, 1999). Secondly we have noted that while initiation is by smoking the switch to injecting through time is the norm. Given the dire consequences of such a transition (Griffiths *et al.*, 1994) again we see a target for early interventions.

Conclusion

These unrepresentative, qualitative community studies fall short on the measures of scientific rigour we would apply to the longitudinal studies and evaluations discussed earlier. They are just as important, however, if we are concerned with developing an effective drugs strategy both to better manage problem drug use but also to 'read' and forecast what lies ahead and thus be better prepared to manage UK Drugs.

In the absence of routine monitoring and an early warning system the national audit of the heroin 'spread' situation in England and Wales was a useful overview. It suggests there is a second 'cycle' of heroin outbreaks underway but in new geographical areas – especially small cities and towns in the regions. The old heroin cities, as yet, report no easily recognizable rise in incidence. The audit identifies several regions such as Yorkshire where these outbreaks are clustering suggesting the epidemiological models of diffusion continue to be useful. As with the 1980s we should not expect the new cycle to affect 'everywhere', just certain regions.

The profile of the new young heroin users outlined by the audit is mirrored in this interview study. Social malaise and far from ideal childhoods continue to be related to heroin use but not in the rather unidirectional way the 'vulnerable groups' agenda would have it. We are seeing – as an unwanted consequence of the normalisation of recreational use – the inadequacy of drugs education, the purposeful supplying of heroin to new areas (Parker *et al.*, 1998a) and the early onset of risk taking among British youth – heroin trying and for some, repeated use on the increase. While only a small minority of young people will ever try heroin, we will find more conforming, bonded, conventional adolescents have become involved as they 'present' during the new decade.

Their voluntary presentation, or alternatively, eventual 'capture' in the criminal justice system will tend to be when they have developed serious poly drug careers. We have seen the worrying coming together of heroin and crack cocaine, the move to injecting and the social realignment of these new users, alas, to the social margins. If they did not begin in the social exclusion zones this is where their drugs journeys leave them five years down the line.

While early interventions would not turn all these unwanted journeys around there is sufficient evidence from this study to suggest that such secondary prevention initiatives are worthy of trialing. Currently they are noticeable by their absence and barely a footnote in the drugs strategy.

Finally, in terms of forecasting, this study reminds us of the dynamics of the heavy end of UK drugs. The new heroin users at the millennium are not quite the same as those found in the last cycle. In particular age of onset has fallen, geographical location has changed and crack cocaine has become a likely secondary drug as heroin careers unfold. In the next chapter we revisit this unholy alliance by looking at crack cocaine careers and the differences between the first and second 'waves' of crack users.

7
Untreatable? Hidden Crack Cocaine and Poly Drug Users

Kevin Brain, Howard Parker and Tim Bottomley

Purpose

Unlike in the USA crack cocaine use has not grown in epidemic fashion in the UK. Its prevalence instead has spread and grown gradually during the 1990s, mainly in the English cities. After heroin, crack or rock cocaine is the drug most associated with the UK's social exclusion zones and 'classic' drugs–crime lifestyles. Just as heroin use can lead on to crack and poly drug use so, as we shall see, regular rock use can also lead into expensive poly drug habits.

In this chapter we describe a two stage ethnographic study of hidden crack cocaine, poly drug users. Most subjects in this investigation have become enemies of the state: they pay few bills, no taxes and indulge in benefit frauds, drug dealing, prostitution and extensive acquisitive crime. They do not trust outsiders and will have no truck with household surveys or traditional research interviews. To 'capture' their accounts and describe their lifestyles requires unconventional research methods. In this community study we employed indigenous fieldworkers who had privileged access into heavy drugs scenes in their own neighbourhoods around Greater Manchester in north west England.

We immediately recognize these highly problematic drugs careers as the stereotypical underbelly of UK drugs and the primary target of the government's drugs strategy. This is the very population which must be successfully engaged through the criminal justice and penal systems if the aspirational goals of reducing Class A drug use and drug related crime in favour of healthy conforming lifestyles are to be achieved.

Qualitative community studies of hidden drugs scenes can also help us forecast change by providing us with clues and cues about how, in this case, the heavy end is evolving. This investigation thus also alerts us to the dangers of crack cocaine spreading into the serious end of recreational drug use.

Crack Cocaine Prevalence in the UK

The dire consequences of crack cocaine use in American cities across the 1980–95 period (Inciardi, 1994; Johnson *et al.*, 1994) suggested that a crack cocaine 'era' is somehow epidemologically related to both the heroin cycle and a period of 'recreational' cocaine powder use (Jacobs, 1999; Johnson, 1999). Yet in the UK the 1980s heroin outbreaks were followed by neither a cocaine scene nor crack cocaine epidemic. So despite a flurry of concern and warnings from American visitors (Kleber, 1988; Stutman, 1989) the research which immediately followed (Bean and Pearson, 1992; Stimson *et al.*, 1993) found only small pockets of use and no evidence of rapid spread.

However, across the decade there were more and more signs and anecdotal or incidental accounts that crack cocaine was finding its way into the sex industry established problem drug arenas and into inner cities in particular (Hunter *et al.*, 1995; McCauley, 1994). Crack/poly drug users were also beginning to emerge in treatment caseloads (Donmall *et al.*, 1996; Gossop *et al.*, 1994) and in the urine testing of arrestees (Bennett, 1998).

The picture at the new decade is of the incremental spread of crack cocaine availability and use in all the English urban centres from Sheffield in the north east to Bristol in the south west, but with few signs, so far, of strong availability in Scotland or Wales. However there is real 'vagueness' in our knowledge base and in the absence of monitoring and research this remains, as we discussed in Chapter 6, a major handicap for both forecasting new developments and, more worryingly, responding to 'hidden' drugs realities.

One way of overcoming this knowledge deficit is with community–street level research studies. The project described here is one of the few qualitative, community level studies of crack cocaine use undertaken in recent years. It involved two periods of fieldwork. In 1995, 63 'hidden' crack cocaine users were located and interviewed (plus a comparison group of 20 heroin users from the same communities). In 1997 the crack users were followed up and 50 were successfully reinterviewed. A further group (n = 29) of new to crack users, again from the same communities, were interviewed for the first time (see Parker and Bottomley, 1996; Brain, Parker and Bottomley, 1998). We begin by summarizing the atypical methodology employed.

Challenging Methods

There is a small but vibrant community of researchers who explore these hidden drugs worlds in both the USA and Europe. They have used a variety of techniques from participant observation to 'snowballing' interviewing and, as in this investigation, relying on indigenous field-workers or privileged access interviewers (Griffiths *et al.*, 1993). The six indigenous fieldworkers (five male, two describing themselves as being black British and four as white British) all lived in the communities in Greater Manchester where the study took place. This team was originally put together via their commonality as clients of a local drugs service. They were, right across the 1995–98 period, a stable network who undertook this and several other smaller, related research projects particularly in respect of the service needs of crack cocaine users.

The team was extensively trained in respect of interviewing techniques and fully involved in the development and piloting of the interview schedule. One training day involved role play through interviewing each other using the schedule. The researchers also provided regular supervision and support for the fieldworkers, seeing them after each interview and checking their completed schedules. Because so many of the potential interviewees they were to contact were heavy end poly drug users and involved in serious crime and drug supplying, health and safety remained a key factor throughout. The fieldworkers were encouraged not to put themselves at risk and their research activities were also 'cleared' with the local police in case they were caught up in a raid or arrest situation.

Both interviewers and interviewees were paid. The fieldworker paid the subject upon completion of the interview. The fieldworker was paid upon each satisfactorily completed and checked schedule and also given the fee for the next respondent. The interviews in both phases were undertaken in either the interviewer's or interviewee's home.

Clearly there are substantive issues of reliability and validity with this technique. Attempts to check interviewees' responses were made using repeat questions within the schedule and in particular obtaining financial estimates of drugs bills in different ways. In the original study a section of the interview was also tape recorded thereby ensuring the interviews took place appropriately. The de-briefing after each interview allowed the lead researchers to scrutinise and discuss each completed schedule and in a few cases further questioning of the respondent was encouraged.

Finally it is important to recognize that the drugs bills' estimates we refer to in this chapter are exactly that. One of the salutary findings about crack cocaine use, including if it is part of a more complex poly drugs repertoire, is that the amounts imbibed vary through time. The interviewees would binge then rest or would find themselves without any funds or suddenly arrested. The drugs consumption diary approach utilized can do no more than generate reasonable estimates of, in particular, past six month consumption patterns based on past week calculations, past month and past six month estimates.

This research technique clearly has the potential to go badly wrong and is most certainly not a cheap and easy approach, especially if conducted competently with due attention to quality checks, health and safety and a timetable. We were fortunate to get through the original study with no foul-ups. At the beginning of the follow up however one of the fieldworkers was arrested and briefly imprisoned. This meant that almost all his confidential contacts (n = 11) were lost and thus not recaptured in the follow up, given that we had purposefully not put names and addresses on the schedules or held a data base with contact details.

Evolving Crack Careers

Background characteristics

The original 1995 sample of crack users consisted of 40 men and 23 women and a similar balance was maintained in the 1997 recaptured sample with 30 being men and 20 women. Looking at ethnic background, the original sample contained 79 per cent white British, 3 per cent white non British, 11 per cent black British, 5 per cent non black British and 2 per cent Asian. The overall profile was largely undisturbed at reinterview, with the corresponding percentages being 82 per cent white British, 6 per cent white non British, 10 per cent black British and 2 per cent Asian.

The vast majority of the original sample had extensive poly drug histories and had come to crack via pre-existing opiate careers. They had the characteristic marginal socio-economic status of dependent opiate users who tend to come from the most socially excluded groups and areas. The vast majority of the original sample was dependent on state benefits and this was still the case for the recaptured sample, as shown in Table 7.1.

The interviewees reported considerable change in their households with partners moving into or out of cohabitation as, often strained, relationships broke down or were rested. The overall picture in terms of actual housing status remains largely unchanged, however, with just under

Table 7.1   Employment and benefit status

	1995 (n = 63)%	1997 (n = 50)%
Income Support	59 (n = 37)	58 (n = 29)
Unemployed no benefits	5 (n = 3)	4 (n = 2)
Sickness/Invalidity	5 (n = 3)	22 (n = 11)
Full-time work	13 (n = 8)	14 (n = 7)
Part-time work	2 (n = 1)	0
Casual work	2 (n = 1)	0
Education/Training	2 (n = 1)	0
Income Support/Casual work	3 (n = 2)	0
Income Support/Part-time work	5 (n = 3)	0
UB/Sickness/Invalidity	5 (n = 3)	0
UB Education/Training	2 (n = 1)	0

Notes: From 1997 missing = 1.
Figures/percentages rounded in most tables.

half living in a council or rented house or flat, a quarter living with parents or relatives and the remainder in temporary or fluid living arrangements.

Alcohol and tobacco use

Table 7.2 outlines the alcohol use status of the original and reinter-viewed samples. We can see that by the time of the second study in 1997 there was a clearly defined polarisation with more of the cohort becoming regular heavy drinkers but also more not using alcohol at all. There appear to be two processes at work here. As we will see, some of the cohort had given up crack use and cut down on their combination illicit drug use but had also switched or returned to heavy frequent drinking. We also have a subgroup of continuing rock users who increasingly used alcohol as a secondary drug to help mediate the effects

Table 7.2   Alcohol use in 1995 and 1997

	1995 (n = 63)%	1997 (n = 50)%
Regular heavy	6 (n = 4)	24 (n = 12)
Occasional heavy	21 (n = 13)	2 (n = 1)
Moderate	16 (n = 10)	10 (n = 5)
Light	14 (n = 9)	4 (n = 2)
Rarely drink	21 (n = 13)	0
Non drinkers	22 (n = 14)	60 (n = 30)

of heavy cocaine use. On the other hand, the rejection of alcohol found classically in a problem drug career is also repeated.

Tobacco use remained central to this small cohort as it did in 1995. Ninety per cent of the interviewees smoked everyday, the average number of cigarettes being consumed each day was 22. Some research suggests nicotine increases craving in crack smokers (Reid *et al.*, 1998).

Crack careers two years on

A fascinating picture of continuity and change emerges as we trace the development of the crack sample's drug careers in the two years between the first study and follow up.

During the in-depth interviews the subjects completed detailed drugs consumption diaries. These diaries reconstructed the previous week, month and six months of drug taking. The consumption diaries, along with more general reflections by the respondents on their patterns of their drug taking over the past six months, were used to construct their recent drugs careers. Clearly, over a period such as six months there will inevitably be variation in drug consumption patterns. However, once we had accounted for this, looking at the overall trends in use and the purposeful choices that were being made by users to continue or review their drug careers, then it became clear that recognizable pathways had developed.

As Figure 7.1 shows of the 50 users in the recaptured cohort, five said they had given up all illegal drugs, eight had stopped using crack in particular, 15 had taken steps to reduce their crack consumption and 22 had continued to use crack and other drugs heavily. Based on these findings it was possible to pick out three pathways: a group who have quit the drug – *the reformed rockheads*; a group attempting to reduce use – *reforming rockheads*; and the *resolute rockheads* who have maintained their crack cocaine lifestyle.

To be a reformed rockhead, interviewees' drug consumption diaries had to record no crack use in the previous month, could only record crack use once in the other five months and had to be accompanied by the user specifically stating that they had given up crack use. To count as a reforming rock head, drug diaries had to show declining amounts of consumption over the six month period and be accompanied by the user purposefully moving towards moderating or giving up crack cocaine over a sustained period.

The reforming pathway category was the hardest to estimate precisely because consumption patterns varied so much. In judging whether or not a user was cutting down we aired on the side of caution. Looking at the number of days crack users actually took crack in the month prior

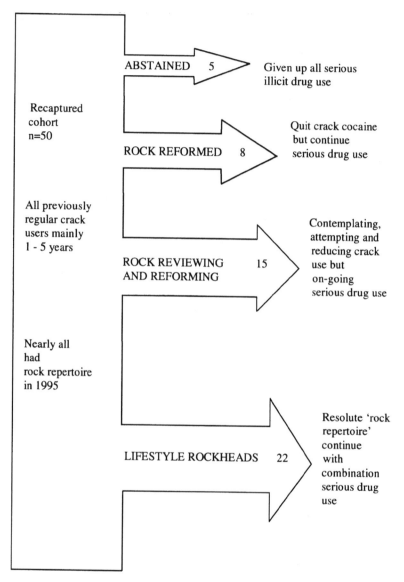

Figure 7.1   Drugs pathways between 1995 and 1997

to the interviews 13 of the 37 continuing crack users only used between nought and seven days. Twenty one however reported using between 13 and 21 days. The remaining three had used between eight and 12 days.

This frequency of use calculation seemed to provide support for the notion that the current users' sample contained a cluster, overall about a third, who could reasonably be described as reforming. Indeed, four of the reforming rockheads had reported using crack only four times in the past six months.

These crack careers reveal a picture of continuity and change. We shall speculate on what might influence the 'flow' of crack careers later. Next we focus our attention on how these diverse crack careers were accompanied by key changes in other areas of drug consumption, expenditure and funding methods.

Changing crack careers and the rock repertoire

The first study, in 1995, coined the term 'rock repertoire' to describe the extensive drugs menu orbiting around crack use. Indeed, distinguishing between crack and heroin as the primary drug of dependency was tenuous for many of the original sample. Not only did many of them have opiate backgrounds prior to crack use but there was also a strong connection between crack use and subsequent use of depressant drugs to manage the 'wired effect' of imbibing crack and help 'come down'. Heroin and methadone figured prominently here as did use of high strength alcohol, cannabis and tranquillisers.

Unsurprisingly with distinctive pathways being taken, the poly drug repertoires of this sample also change. We can see from Table 7.3 that changes in crack consumption correlate with changes in heroin (eight had stopped using whilst three others had taken it up) and methadone (six had quit but 12 begun). Cannabis remains popular with and important to half the sample, while dance drugs have little attraction.

Table 7.3 Drug use patterns and pathways since 1995 (n = 50)

	Use in 1995 Quit by 1997 (%)	Use in both 1995 and 1997 (%)	Began using since 1995 (%)	Not used at all 1995–97 (%)
Rock cocaine	26 (n = 13)	74 (n = 47)	N/A	N/A
Heroin	16 (n = 8)	58 (n = 29)	6 (n = 3)	20 (n = 10)
Methadone	12 (n = 6)	24 (n = 12)	24 (n = 12)	40 (n = 20)
Cannabis	10 (n = 5)	48 (n = 24)	2 (n = 1)	40 (n = 20)
Ecstasy	8 (n = 4)	4 (n = 2)	0	88 (n = 44)
Speed	2 (n = 1)	0	4 (n = 2)	94 (n = 47)
LSD	2 (n = 1)	0	0	98 (n = 49)
Minor tranquillisers	16 (n = 8)	2 (n = 1)	4 (n = 2)	78 (n = 39)

The reformed rockheads were unsurprisingly also the most successful in moderating their overall drugs consumption. The eight of the 13 who continued serious drug use were reporting reductions in quantity and frequency particularly in respect of heroin which five had also stopped using.

The reforming and resolute rockheads continued to be heavy combination drug users, particularly of crack, heroin and/or methadone. As we shall see, this ensured that enormous drug bills continued to ring up. There was no predictable pattern in terms of how reducing crack use affected heroin and/or methadone use.

> I don't use heroin anymore, just methadone and my rock is only when I'm flushed. (Case 1, male, aged 34)
> Stone is a luxury drug now, will buy it if we're flushed. It's bad enough having a gear habit...those days of trying to keep the candle burning at both ends are in the past. (Case 7, female, aged 30)
> I hardly use crack anymore. I use an awful lot of heroin. (Case 20, female, aged 26)

However the resolute rockheads remained deeply committed to and entrenched in the rock repertoire lifestyles.

> I never ever go without rock and now that I don't have to sort my boyfriend (in prison) I don't have to. I never go without even when I cannot get my gear for a few hours. I will still buy a rock knowing I will feel like tearing my hair out once it is finished and I have to wait for the gear....I will stay on crack, heroin, methadone and prozac but will try and get a lot more prozac because I can be out of my face all the time...they have a really calming effect. (Case 34, female, aged 32)
> Methadone is sometimes a real life saver because when I have no money for gear then I can take my meth, buy charlie and I know I won't be ill and can still enjoy the charlie without a worry in the world. (Case 36, female, aged 32)
> Rock is the most important. I would probably use more heroin if I stopped rock. Rock takes up the first £40 of the day unless I'm withdrawing badly from heroin. (Case 50, male, aged 24)

Rock Repertoires, Drug Bills and Drug Crime Connections

The original study had been commissioned in the wake of the 'moral panic' around crack use, crime and the degeneration of the urban ghettoes

Table 7.4   Total drugs bill over six month period 1995 and 1997

	1995 (n = 63)%	*1997* (n = 50)%
£0	0	8 (n = 4)
£240–£1000	5 (n = 3)	16 (n = 8)
£1001–£3000	16 (n = 10)	16 (n = 8)
£3001–£6000	21 (n = 13)	20 (n = 10)
£6001–£10 000	22 (n = 14)	14 (n = 7)
£10 001–£20 000	13 (n = 8)	10 (n = 5)
£20 001–£30 000	5 (n = 3)	2 (n = 1)
£30 001–£65 000	6 (n = 4)	12 (n = 6)
£71 000	0	2 (n = 1)
Using for < 6 months	6 (n = 4)	
Missing/unclear	6 (n = 4)	

in the USA. A key aim of the 1995 phase was to investigate the relationship between crack consumption and crime.

Maintaining a crack career and a rock repertoire is prohibitively expensive. For the original sample yearly drug bills ranged from £6000 to over £60 000 with the average being just over £20 000. Similarly, when recontacted this sample still had average yearly drug bills of around £20 000. The drug bills of the sample were calculated using the past week, past month and past six months drugs consumption diaries' calculations. The six monthly totals are outlined in Table 7.4. Given the expense involved in maintaining a poly drugs career, the success or otherwise of reducing crack consumption played a crucial role in determining the overall cost of the recaptured sample's drug lifestyles and their ability to reduce their involvement in acquisitive crime.

With the reformed rockheads being the most successful in bringing down their overall drug bills they are responsible for the major reductions found at the less than £1001 cut off. Given the fact that the vast majority of the 37 resolute or reforming rockheads also used heroin, drug bills for these two groups are inevitably very high. A crack user (in 1997) using one rock per day (£20), one bag of brown (heroin – £10) and smoking cannabis throughout the day (£10) would run up a weekly drug bill of £280.00. In reality drugs consumption rates vary across a year but for the record such a constant weekly bill would produce a yearly drug total of £14 000.

The actual average bill for the recaptured cohort was just over £20 000 a year. This is because the reductions produced by the quitters have been more than countered by the very high drug bills of the lifestyle 'rock repertoire' users. Drug prices appeared to have remained stable between the two study periods.

Funding expensive habits

The original study found that these users relied on a range of income sources – wages, benefits, dealing, gifts from partners and others, borrowing, indebtedness, drug dealing, prostitution and acquisitive crime. However, becoming embroiled in dependent crack use both increased offending rates for many of those users whose criminal careers predated crack use and, for the 22 who did not have a criminal career predating their crack use, over two-thirds subsequently turned to acquisitive crime, drug dealing or prostitution.

At the two year follow up the same range of funding strategies was still being used by the recaptured sample. Table 7.5 describes the strategies used to finance their drug lifestyles. There is a shift towards state benefits primarily because, two years on, fewer of the sample have waged jobs and more are now eligible for sickness/invalidity benefits and also undertake casual work while still claiming benefits. The general picture at 1995 and 1997 is, unsurprisingly, very similar in that there are few other realistic methods available for people without savings or capital to raise drug money. The reduction in 'partner' provision is a consequence of drug using couples splitting up, often as a consequence of disagreements about drug use or one party being incarcerated.

Table 7.6 shows the relative significance of these different income sources and funding strategies. The most important income source remains acquisitive crime followed by drug dealing and prostitution.

There are real difficulties in interpreting the drugs → crime, crime → drugs relationships in this sample, given the problems of recollection about

Table 7.5 All funding strategies of illegal drug use 1995 and 1997

	1995 (n = 63) (%)	*1997* (n = 45) (%)
Benefits	65 (n = 41)	89 (n = 40)
Wages	19 (n = 12)	9 (n = 4)
Casual work	10 (n = 6)	24 (n = 11)
Dealing	43 (n = 27)	34 (n = 14)
Prostitution	17 (n = 11)	16 (n = 7)
Gifts/Partner supplies	43 (n = 27)	20 (n = 9)
Loans	24 (n = 15)	20 (n = 9)
Acquisitive crime	51 (n = 32)	47 (n = 21)

Table 7.6 Main sources of funding illegal drugs bills 1995 and 1997

	1995 (n = 63) %	1997 (n = 45) %
Wages	8 (n = 4)	7 (n = 3)
Benefits	4 (n = 2)	11 (n = 5)
Casual work	8 (n = 4)	11 (n = 5)
Dealing	8 (n = 4)	16 (n = 7)
Prostitution	18 (n = 9)	16 (n = 7)
Crime	24 (n = 12)	24 (n = 11)
Gifts	16 (n = 8)	6 (n = 3)
Dealing/crime	12 (n = 6)	4 (n = 2)
Crime/gifts	2 (n = 1)	0
Dealing/Casual work	0	2 (n = 1)
Crime/Loans	0	2 (n = 1)

mid adolescence. What is clear is that within the overall sample, while a majority had delinquent episodes prior to any significant drug use, a minority clearly believe that their crack–poly drugs careers have pulled them into overlapping drugs–crime careers. They blame their heavy drug use for their criminality. In summary, the strong evidence that entrenched poly drug careers do generate, not just acquisitive crime but also drug dealing and sex industry work, is consistent with the wider research literature. We can see this relationship not just in the funding strategies of the resolute rockheads but in the reductions in acquisitive crime among the reformers.

These lifestyle poly drug users are clearly a key target in the new UK drugs strategy. Their drugs consumption is linked to their propensity to commit crime. Indeed, despite most of the on-going users agreeing that they only got apprehended for a very small proportion of their offending and despite the interviewed drug dealers avoiding detection, no less than 56 per cent of the sample (28) had received convictions in the two intervening years. No fewer than 30 per cent of the overall sample were awaiting 'serious' court hearings which many anticipated would lead to a period of custody. Despite all this only three of the 28 reported any kind of treatment or counselling 'drugs' intervention. In part this is because respondents saw no value in disclosing their drugs status but more often was indicative of the criminal justice system not having been geared up for such interventions during the 1990s. The new drugs strategy will need to target and work with drug using offenders such as these if it is to achieve its goals of providing effective treatment through community correction and prison programmes.

All this said, we must remember that the drugs–crime relationships are complex and diverse and that focusing on drug use as a sole driver of crime will only have limited success.

> For the first year or so I was nicking everything for it and all the money I made out of selling it went back on stone . . . I would nick anything I thought I could sell . . . since I got a script and stopped using white I don't rob anything anymore I'm just trying to get my life back together. (Case 19, male, aged 23)
>
> Now I wake up and I go out shoplifting and I don't come back in until I've got enough for at least a stone and a bag and then I'll be out again once or twice more. (Case 21, male, aged 27)
>
> I doubt if I would be selling as much now if I did not have a crack habit. I would more than likely be settled down with my ex and a couple of children. (Case 11, male, aged 22)
>
> For the last 4 to 5 years its been the same. I had to steal for my heroin habit anyway but I do a lot more for rock. (Case 9, male, aged 22).
>
> I would be committing crime (burglary) anyway. It's just that I've chose to spend the proceeds on drugs. (Case 9, male, aged 22)
>
> I know loads of blokes who don't dabble and are robbing night and day so I can't blame my drug use for that (my crime). I would be a dead end kid even if I didn't take drugs. (Case 5, male, aged 34)

Moreover there are other ways of funding an expensive drugs habit which largely avoid detection but nevertheless undermine personal and community reputations. We found prostitution and drug dealing were routinely utilized and that the 'misuse' of benefits also often undermined domestic and parenting responsibilities. It is highly unlikely that, without accompanying robust social inclusion strategies, criminal justice interventions will address the wider social costs of crack cocaine lifestyles.

Contemplating and Affecting 'reform'

In this section we focus on the factors which appear to influence whether this sample maintain their drugs–crime lifestyles or modify their use of heavy end drugs.

One of the clearest messages of both the 1995 and 1997 studies is that a rock lifestyle is incredibly difficult to sustain. There are the obvious difficulties of financing consumption and the risks that go along with many of the illegal funding strategies adopted. There are also the obviously corrosive effects a rock lifestyle seems to have on users' social and family relationships and their ability to fulfil the demands of day to day living. It is striking that the majority of the 1997 recaptured sample thought that there was virtually nothing positive about being on crack and living a life around the drug. It was a drug that exacted too many demands.

> I hated the lying to everyone including myself. . . . I can honestly say there isn't anything good about crack. (Case 12, female, aged 21)
>
> They (family) won't lend me money anymore. I could get thrown out any day . . . they are giving me loads about money and drugs, its never been so bad. (Case 40, male, aged 26)
>
> If I don't stop using I'll be dead. I feel like killing myself I can't handle it . . . need help. (Case 45, male, aged 32)
>
> There's nothing good about it. It just fucks your life, swallows your money and kills your pride. (Case 24, female, aged 22)
>
> The way you have no time for anyone, your family and child and all the effort you have to put into getting the drugs. (Case 25, female, aged 28)

Two thirds of the reforming and resolute rockheads reported health problems. The main problems here were bad chests and breathing difficulties, deterioration in skin texture and appearance and feeling paranoid and agitated. Added to this there are also the difficulties of being seen as the lowest of the low even within the subterranean worlds of dependent drug users.

> We don't seem to get no respect off most dealers because they see us as the scum of the earth. (Case 32, female, aged 27)

However, crack is also seen as being an intensely pleasurable drug to take which leaves users craving more and chasing the buzz of the first rock. A consistent finding of both the 1995 and 1997 studies was that crack was considered to be a particularly 'moreish' drug which induces cravings and, in this sense, was regarded as being psychologically, more than physically, addictive.

> It has always been a fight when you've got money but it has never been your body that wants it. (Case 26, male, aged 28)
>
> It's like when its in your head you can't move it. You're even thinking about tomorrow's use before you've got through today. (Case 26, male, aged 28)

Table 7.7 Length of time of crack use and crack pathways

	'Reformed' (n = 13) %	'Reforming' (n = 15) %	'Resolute' (n = 22) %
Four years and under	77 (n = 10)	40 (n = 6)	27 (n = 6)
Over four years	23 (n = 3)	60 (n = 9)	72 (n = 16)

In particular, the longer the period of use the more likely users seemed to be to attribute feelings of psychological dependency. The length of use and perceptions of dependency were related to the success our recaptured sample had in becoming reformed rockheads. Of the 13 users who had reformed and given up crack, nearly ten had done so *before* they had used crack for over four years. By contrast, of the 22 resolute users only six had used for less than four years.

Although we are dealing with very small numbers it does seem as though we can distinguish between 'lifestyle', 'rockhead' cum poly drug users who are unable or unwilling to give serious consideration to giving up crack cocaine and those who, if they are able to contemplate change in the first few years of the rock repertoire, can pull away from crack and to some extent the accompanying combination drug use. For the drug users in this study it seemed that the following three factors combined to facilitate the contemplation or actualisation of change.

- a growing unwillingness or inability to cope with the difficulties of sustaining crack use;
- a significant life event that led to a change in lifestyle;
- the ability to rely on supportive significant others.

Where these combined we were far more likely to see 'reform'.

> I tried to stop using stone and gear while she was pregnant but I never could properly and then when I got locked up I had no choice. Some mates would sort me out when they could but it wasn't enough for the habit I had. I didn't have no money inside so I roasted . . . when I got out my partner had stopped and helped me. (Case 15, male, aged 25)
>
> I got into loads of debt, lost quite a few mates and nearly lost my family all because of the drugs. It was all going too far and had been for a while. If it didn't stop I would have ended up on me own somewhere or in jail for years. (Case 19, male, aged 41)

> When I got my dog I was seeing how much I was wasting every time. I bought that shit for a five to ten minute buzz, and I just ended up sacking it. Now I walk about eight miles a day with the dog and spend most of my money on outdoor wear. . . . I just saw what a waste it was of my time, efforts and money so I stopped. (Case 18, male, aged 31)

The resolute rockheads are more fatalistic and less questioning.

> I know it sounds wet but there is no way apart from prison that any-one, even my mum, could stop me from taking stone. . . . If I couldn't take drugs I wouldn't want to live. (Case 5, male, aged 34)
>
> I have gone without probably at most for three quarters of a day when I have been to see my children or my mother. But the minute I leave them I arrange to score on the way home and stop off in (fast food chain's) toilets and have a good few big pipes to pat myself on the back for being unselfish for a short while. (Case 31, male, aged 29)
>
> I have just got used to taking it and I could not function, do my business without a smoke. Speaking for myself, it keeps me alert and on top of things. I know it always gets bad shit wrote about it but they are hardly going to say crack is great. (Case 12, male, aged 25)

New Recruits and New Crack Careers – Continuity and Change

Diverse characteristics

As part of the follow up study we also recruited 29 'new' crack cocaine users to see if their crack careers were similar to the 'first wave' of British crack users. The new users, people who had started using crack in the second half of the 1990s, came from the same communities as the original sample. Although a higher percentage were in employment (24 per cent as against 14 per cent) the vast majority, like their contemporaries in the original samples, were on benefit and from similar socio-economic backgrounds. We must emphasize that we cannot be sure how represent-ative of new crack users this sample is, even from the region in question. This said, there are some noticeable differences between these newer users and our original cohort. Moreover, some of the characteristics and drug taking patterns of the new users suggest that important processes of change are underway in respect of the range of people who will try or use crack, and, as a consequence, the image and spread potential of the drug.

Table 7.8   Pre-cocaine drugs histories of new user and original cohort compared

	1995 (n = 63) %	*1997* (n = 29) %
	Ever tried	Ever tried
Cannabis	92 (n = 58)	97 (n = 28)
Solvent/Gas	29 (n = 18)	24 (n = 7)
Mushrooms	52 (n = 33)	24 (n = 7)
LSD	65 (n = 41)	35 (n = 10)
Amphetamines	76 (n = 48)	62 (n = 18)
Ecstasy	63 (n = 40)	55 (n = 16)
Tranquillisers	65 (n = 41)	35 (n = 10)
Heroin	71 (n = 45)	41 (n = 12)
Methadone	49 (n = 31)	31 (n = 9)

As with the original 1995 sample, our new users had extensive drug careers encompassing nearly all the widely available street drugs. The key difference was that the majority of the new sample had non-opiate backgrounds whereas with the original 1995 sample the majority had used heroin. The early drug backgrounds of the new users corresponded with those now routinely found in young recreational user populations described in earlier chapters. This is an important finding because it suggests that, in addition to recruitment from the traditional heavy end heroin and methadone drug careerists, new pathways into rock cocaine may have opened up.

Overall the new recruits tended to be lighter users than the original sample, 17 of them used less than seven rocks a week. The other cluster, of 12, who used more than seven rocks per week had a profile very similar to the original cohort. They were far more likely to have larger rock repertoires. These included heroin and methadone. They were highly pessimistic about their ability to control their rock use.

> I'm addicted to it when I've got no money ... I want to sack it off but when I've got money I can't help myself. (Case 21, male, aged 27)

This pattern of an increasing sense of psychological addiction with prolonged use has been found in the original, recapture and new user interviews. We are not suggesting there is any inevitability about this process. Indeed users are probably defining the term addiction in a variety of ways. However, the increasing sense of losing control over crack consumption and an associated fatalist view of the rock lifestyle stems from a recognition of rock's moreishness.

Table 7.9 The rock repertoire: taking other drugs alongside crack (n = 29)

	(a) Number of other drugs (%)	(b) Key drugs utilized (%)
0/1	45 (n = 13)	Cannabis 55 (n = 16)
2/3	48 (n = 14)	Heroin 28 (n = 11)
4/5	7 (n = 2)	Methadone 28 (n = 8)
		Amphetamines 14 (n = 4)
		Tranquillisers 7 (n = 2)

One identifiable cluster in this sample also displayed the tendency to use a range of depressant drugs, primarily heroin and methadone, to manage the 'wired effect' and 'come down' from crack. The main combinations for these newer users were crack and heroin; crack, heroin and methadone; and crack, heroin and cannabis. Most of the methadone used by these newer users was bought from the illicit market. This cluster also employed the same range of funding strategies as the original cohort, with length of use predicting increasing reliance on illegal funding strategies. Their rock repertoire careers either amplified previous criminal activities or triggered acquisitive crime.

> You start off by having fun with it so that's what you remember and want that fun again. (Case 14, female, aged 20)
> From when you have the first pipe you know things are going to happen. (Case N9, male, aged 22)
> It just stays in your head from the last pipe of the night until the first in the morning. (Case 8, male, aged 20)
> It's hard once it's in your head and a few mates come round. So you might as well do the act and get it done. (Case 16, male, aged 24)
> You'd have to do it a lot more than I do for quite a long time before you get addicted? (Pause) Wouldn't you? (Case 22, female, aged 19)

As with the original cohort the new users were more likely to regard themselves as psychologically dependent on crack the longer they had been using. Fourteen of the new users regarded themselves as addicted; twelve of these said this was a psychological dependency, one a physical addiction and one both physical and psychological. Ten of the 14 who regarded themselves as being addicted had been using crack for more than six months. By contrast only three of the 15 who did not regard themselves as addicted in any way had been using for more than six months.

New Pathways into Crack Cocaine Careers

In terms of demonstrating the potential 'forecasting' value of small ethno-graphic 'community' studies, we shall concentrate here on one cluster – the new younger crack takers who see themselves as 'recreational' users. This small, unrepresentative sample can offer no rough guide to regional prevalence rates but the fact that this group were easily identi-fied by our indigenous fieldworkers as a recognizable type of new user is nevertheless instructional. The interviewees themselves had spotted the changing pathways into, and profiles of, the new crack or to borrow their preferred term 'stone' users. The older rockheads noted:

> They're the kind of person who years ago looked at you as if you were shit. (Crack N27, male, aged 29)
> The people I know seem to be more stable straightheads. Both I know are white girls in their mid twenties with their own gaffs. (Case N39, female, aged 33)

Their non opiate backgrounds distinguish them from the first wave of the early 1990s.

> ...that's hard to say but they seem to be first time drug users. By first time users I mean they don't do heroin. They are young.... Case N6, female, aged 24)
> More black guys seem to use it and young people with a heroin background...more people that use uppers. I think more younger people will experiment with it and there won't be so many heavy users. (Case N20, female, aged 26)
> I have never had more than one stone on any given day...have no intention of letting drugs become anything but recreational.... Went to Ireland six weeks ago and never thought of it (crack) once. (Case N2, male, aged 17)
> I don't smoke in mid week when I'm working, only weekends.... There is no way I would let the drug dictate when I take it. If I thought I was changing I would knock it on the head. (Case N4, male, aged 24)
> I don't know a lot of dealers or crack users. I stick to a small band of intimate friends and would never try and score off the streets. (Case N7, female, aged 18)
> Although I am not, and I mean it, addicted in any way, I think my boyfriend may be, psychologically, you know dependent on it. (Case 7, female, aged 18)

I don't have it enough but it is highly addictive and if I didn't control it I'd be (psychologically) addicted to it. (Case N19, male, aged 27)

However when we assess their reassuring accounts against the careers of all the other interviewees especially in the recaptured sample, we must doubt their self confidence. The consistent picture of dependency increasing with length of use must cast real doubts on whether they can all maintain tight control over their rock cocaine use. Their best prospects are to follow the quitters and reformers and pull away from their 'stone' use within the first couple of years and by distancing themselves from the temptations of being with fellow users.

We are not suggesting they will inevitably become problem users. There is sufficient evidence and a healthy debate about cocaine (Ditton and Hammersley, 1996; *Addiction Research*, 1994) to suggest strong will and rational consumption decisions can keep crack cocaine use in check. However, the prospects of a casualty rate with this sample seem high given their socio-economic circumstances and the continuous availability and presence of 'moreish' drugs in their social worlds.

Discussion

Crack or rock cocaine is highly unlikely to become a widely used drug in the UK. Its price, reputation and dangerous moreishness will ensure that the vast majority of even those who use illicit drugs will eschew it. It will remain a drug primarily associated with the social exclusion zones and with disadvantaged groups. It is slowly spreading into these areas and populations and has found a foothold in most English cities. It has not yet become widely available in the rest of the UK's urban areas. This slow non-epidemic diffusion has been underway right across the 1990s but alas with no on-going research and monitoring we have only a sketchy picture. A major worry must be that as efficient crack cocaine distribution follows the fault lines of social exclusion so it will join heroin and produce simultaneous heroin and crack cocaine and consequently poly drugs careers in our poorer communities. We have seen the consequences of this in both this study and that focusing on young heroin users discussed in Chapter 6.

The development of these highly problematic heavy end careers will sorely stretch and test the drugs strategy. There can be no doubting that the criminal justice and the prison systems will indeed be fruitful sites for intervention. The majority of our main sample have been moving through both on a regular basis. There are even grounds for believing that a significant minority might welcome an official intervention given their regrets about crack cocaine and periods 'roasting' in prison. On the other hand they are an alienated 'anti-authority' group who do not trust the State nor its officials and whose lifestyles were most often neither gestated nor generated by heroin–crack cocaine careers.

We have seen too many care leavers, under-qualified and impoverished respondents (Marlow and Pearson, 1999) whose unbounded and deviant lifestyles pre-dated serious drug use to believe that a drugs 'treatment' intervention alone could turn them into the healthy, law abiding citizens the drugs strategy requires. Here again we must question whether the drugs treatment sector can be sufficiently responsive to reach, gain trust and treat these poly drug users. We would want to see far more robust and integrated intervention packages, well beyond methadone prescribing, prompting stimulant users to present to CDTs and clinics (Donmall *et al.*, 1996; Wright and Klee, 1999) before believing these rock repertoire careers could be challenged successfully. And far more success at regenerating urban centres with high social malaise and youth unemployment would need to be achieved before we can expect those at the margins and from subcultural worlds to conform to the lifestyles the state requires of them.

Turning now to forecasting and thus early interventions, there are important messages from the new users' sample. However small and unrepresentative, the fact that our indigenous fieldworkers easily found a sample of young adults who got into crack cocaine through the 'recreational route', eschewing heroin, is surely indicative. That such young adults saw themselves as 'recreational' users of crack, or 'stone' as some termed it, illustrates how dynamic is the drugs landscape and warns us that 'hard' and 'soft' drugs distinctions are being lost. That we find such use at the same time as cocaine powder consumption is spreading rapidly in the recreational scene (Boys *et al.*, 1998; Ramsay and Partridge, 1999) is a particular cause for concern. In the USA expensive cocaine powder snorting was a precursor to the expansion of crack cocaine use (Johnson, 1999).

In Chapter 8 we will refer to forecasting more formally but this speculative discussion is, we believe, exactly what is notably absent in official thinking. Currently government is largely unresponsive to any deterioration in the drugs landscape. What is required is a monitoring and research agenda which can take up cues such as these and test out the veracity of, in this case, the possibility that in the new decade we may see, not just a significant spread in cocaine powder use, but the development of a small but nevertheless highly problematic crack cocaine population and perhaps residing beyond, as well as within, the main cities. We have even offered the processes, which need to be spotted. The current price of around £20 a rock would need to fall. The imagery of crack would need to soften, probably via new names like 'stone'. The more extensive use of cocaine powder may itself do this by putting another rung in the stimulant ladder after amphetamines and ecstasy. Signs of crack use among the clubbers and twentysomething cocaine users would be highly indicative.

Once one accepts these kinds of outline forecasts can be generated by, in this case, street level research, then government can, as well as monitoring the situation, utilize the time created to prepare early interventions or preventive measures. These might include information and advice to recreational drug users who are, as others have shown, generally responsive to, balanced public information messages (Branigan and Wellings, 1999). 'Say no to smack and crack' or 'step back now if you're craving your stone' are not going to be messages that everyone need hear nor everyone will heed. However, in this case because the large susceptible group, beyond the exclusion zones, are the recreational drug users, then public health messages have some prospect of success. Alas there are no signs of such an approach being developed except through local initiatives, a point will we return to in the final chapter, as we review the national programme and its eventual plans to give greater priority to monitoring and forecasting.

8
Unpredictable? Britain's Drugs Futures

Howard Parker, Judith Aldridge and Roy Egginton

Purpose

We now attempt to draw together the lessons from our cameos of the diverse and complex range of drugs scenes which make up UK drugs. Our primary concern here is policy and 'good practice' development. Our starting point is that the new drugs strategy, as the first real attempt to manage UK drugs, has more integrity and realism than could have been reasonably expected and thus should be the starting point for evolving a robust and more effective management machine. We do have major criticisms to make of the strategy but these are hopefully constructive.

In this chapter we thus have the difficult task of identifying the very real threat to the strategy from forces of conservatism and inherited under investment in the drugs interventions industry while simultaneously suggesting that the strategy itself, despite its strengths, has, by not taking sufficient cognisance of complex drugs realities, in-built fault lines. These will possibly become credibility gaps and indicators of under performance, even failure, over the next few years.

That so much changed and in such dramatic, unexpected fashion across the 1990s leads us to conclude that the shape of the drugs landscape in 2010 is largely unpredictable. What is more predictable is where we will be at the end of New Labour's first administration. Thus, we assess the likelihood of the 'rising' epidemiological trends in recreational and hard drug use we have described turning down, of supply being stifled and treatment delivering, by the next election. For what is also predictable is that *de facto* the national programme will then come under intense scrutiny and its weaknesses become more publicly evident.

The Forces of Conservatism

In this final chapter we try to draw together the lessons from the range of different kinds of drug triers and users and drugs scenes we have explored. Even from this small collection of recent studies it is quite clear that we must recognize that diversity, dynamism and thus complexity dominate. There can be no neat overall, all inclusive descriptions, definitions or projections to describe such a range of drug users and styles of use. We must compare this drugs reality with the picture and assumptions which underpin the UK drugs strategy as part and parcel of our assessment as to its likely efficacy.

However before we can do this we must look more broadly at the historical and political backcloth, because the way UK drugs is managed or indeed neglected is the product of many other forces. Many of these are political being the 'forces of conservatism' found in the war on drugs discourse, the politics of re-election and the consequent lack of sophistication within central and, indeed, local government, in terms of having systems and structures in place to guide any integrated strategy.

The hegemony of the war on drugs discourse is hard to quantify. It has become more subtle in the new decade but it still undermines rational discussion of how UK drugs can be better understood and managed. It inhibits honest, open debate. The most disappointing feature of the discourse is not that it is used by unmoveable, committed evangelical 'warriors' but that it constrains those who actually have understanding and knowledge of today's drugs realities. There is an institutionalised dishonesty at work, not just in politics and among government ministers, but in the civil service and indeed among key players in the relevant professions. In private police officers joke about the fact they should even respond to cannabis possession. DAT co-ordinators privately dismiss the widespread recreational drug use in their area as a 'problem' before filling out their monitoring forms for government, listing all their initiatives to prevent it. Teachers deliver their drugs prevention packages to year 10 before musing in the common room that the 15-year-olds know more about dance drugs than they did and taught them more than the trainer's curriculum notes. Such contradictions are clearly not as invidious as those displayed by journalists, who construct their drugs–crime–death stories with a gram of cocaine in their pocket, but they serve to remind us how widespread are the distortions and, indeed contortions, required to 'officially' deal with drugs. We must unequivocally include ourselves in all this. We too agree to sanitise our reports for government and learn, often from exchanges with civil servants, what can and cannot be said – or be disowned or discredited.

The politics of re-election, by playing to the tabloid galleries with dramatic sound bites about law and order and enhanced enforcement, is a further handicap. Not only are politicians profoundly ignorant about drugs issues but ministers and shadow ministers, who are a little better briefed, will regularly override or undermine sensible, considered policy initiatives in order to impress the voters and deflect any 'soft on drugs' headlines. Because the war on drugs discourse provides the main explanatory framework within the media it is also the way much of the public conceptualise and understand UK drugs. The inevitable political logic is thus to utilize this discourse to win votes. We will see all this recur in 2001 in the build up to the next General Election. In September 1999 Tony Blair, the UK Prime Minister, warmed up. He is 'petrified' of drugs. He believed, he told the Labour Party Conference, in civil liberties 'the liberty of parents to drop their kids off at school without worrying they're dropping them straight into the arms of the drug dealers'. These drug dealers are part of 'the most chilling, evil industry the world has to confront'. (*Daily Mail*, 29 September 1999). The leader of the Conservative opposition responded with a policy proposal to imprison those caught more than once selling drugs to under 16 year olds. Yet when we actually look at how young people obtain drugs (for example Chapter 2) all this becomes a dangerous mischief, an untruth. The 'real' drug dealers who 'pressure' young people as defined by our politicians are in fact young people themselves. The drug 'dealers' at the school gates are the pupils. Imprisoning *them*, while it would reduce class sizes significantly, thereby helping achieve another government goal, is not presumably what either political party had in mind. Clearly to have a drugs 'reality' debate about this conundrum is simply not allowed. Waging the war on drugs against our own children is a rather more explosive agenda to successfully manage.

This subversive approach to publicly discussing drugs is self perpetuating and those who attempt to break its rules can easily be discredited as 'legalisers', anarchists and people who do not care about the damage that can be done by drugs. However, by its very nature this linguistic and ideological hegemony is hard to quantify and its significance impossible to gauge accurately. Our intuitive view, however, is that the combination of institutionalised dishonesty, the war on drugs discourse and the politics of re-election collectively remain a drag anchor on progress towards the more successful management of UK drugs and, consequently, pose a real threat to the survival of the national programme or certainly its potential integrity and evidence based development into an effective arm of government.

The Fate of UK Drugs Strategy

Confusion over target and goal setting

While the usual civil service speak and customary working together with joined-up government statements all suggest that there is a coherent UK drugs strategy, the reality is somewhat different. The traditional separateness of government in Scotland and Northern Ireland, being further reinforced by devolution and with Wales becoming somewhat more freestanding via the Welsh Assembly, means what is presented as the UK Anti-drugs Strategy (for example, Cabinet Office, 1999) is in reality four rather different approaches.

Northern Ireland which has traditionally had far less drug involvement than the rest of the UK has both different governmental and administrative arrangements and a rather less sophisticated response structure. The country has so far never had a hard drug–heroin problem and, thus, has no established treatment structure nor any methadone programmes. Drugs supplying and distribution are tied up in its political troubles via paramilitary 'policing', and its recreational scene although growing remains less prevalent than elsewhere in the UK. The province has its own drugs strategy (Northern Ireland Drugs Campaign, 1999) which, while it follows the general template set in the UK strategy in terms of the four key areas, has two key differences. First, it avoids the war on drugs language steering clear of talk of young people needing to be helped to 'resist' drugs so they can reach their 'full potential'. Instead it talks of providing young people with information and of reducing harm. Second, the strategy completely avoids setting clear targets or outcome measures and indeed talks of reviewing current strategy in 2002 and 2004.

Tackling Drugs in Scotland: Action in Partnership (The Scottish Office, 1999) is similarly free of war talk, placing far more emphasis, overtly, on harm reduction and meeting drug users' needs. In particular, having been pressured to face up to its growing heroin, temazepan problem there are clear government plans to develop early interventions with young problem drug users, including the use of mass media public health messages. Scotland is developing criminal justice interventions including the Treatment and Testing Order and prison based programmes, as in England and Wales, and the emphasis on drug supply and distribution disruption through enforcement is also in place. However again, there are no specific targets and milestones like those found in the 'UK' strategy.

Wales' drugs strategy, which uniquely includes alcohol interventions, is also being reshaped by the politics of the new Assembly. This said, it remains more closely shaped by the dominant 'English' template than in the other two countries.

In conclusion there is an undoubted tension in whether the 'UK' template and performance indicators are actually recognized as binding especially in Scotland and Northern Ireland. Government departments in these countries are distancing themselves, not from the general thrust of the strategy but from the specific aspirational goals and, indeed, the authority of the UK Anti Drugs Co-ordination Unit to intervene. This incoherence is commonplace when Whitehall attempts to create UK compliance, but such inconsistencies will inevitably make the on-going debate about the UK strategy and its progress even more confusing and difficult. Indeed the continuation of current co-ordination arrangements may well be one victim of the politicking

Monitoring and evaluation problems

As we look specifically at the exact targets defined in the overarching UK programme and how appropriate and realistic they are, we have, simultaneously, to give serious consideration to whether we have the research tools and sophisticated monitoring systems to actually evaluate the programme. Once again we find that the indifference of previous administrations and related reactiveness and thus, conservativeness of official responses, are inherited to handicap the future. In short, the measuring tools to evaluate the strategic targets are absent or inadequate and while strenuous efforts to rescue the situation are under way across the 1999–2002 period, the stark reality is that they will not be sufficiently robust or sophisticated to produce a convincing analysis in several target areas. We will elude to this handicap as we discuss each of the four strategic target areas.

Preventing and reducing rates of drug use

The strategy puts much faith in the ability of primary prevention through drugs education in junior and secondary schools and related community programmes with parents. However as we discussed in Chapters 3 and 4 there is little evidence such programmes are effective in reducing drug trying and that, at best, only marginal gains can be expected in reducing drug use (Caulkins *et al.*, 1999; White and Pitts, 1998). This does not mean that present and future early adolescent age cohorts, in the new millennium, will invariably continue the upward prevalence trends found among their 1990s predecessors. Indeed there are good reasons to expect a plateau or a slight fall in *adolescent* drug use at the new decade (Balding, 1999) as was also noted with the new younger cohort in the Northern Regions Longitudinal Study (see Chapter 3). If these 'gains' do indeed occur and, even though generated largely independently of official interventions, they will understandably be seized upon as achievements for the strategy. Yet, even if this does occur the UK will still have one of the most drug involved populations in the post industrialised world.

Whether the 'UK' programme targets will be used to assess the Northern Ireland and Scotland national programmes remains unclear but certainly for England, which anyway embraces the vast majority of the UK population, these outcome measures will be utilized by both the drugs interventions industry itself and the programme's critics. The key performance targets are to reduce all illicit drug use substantially among all under 25 year olds and to reduce the proportion of younger people using heroin and cocaine by 25 per cent by 2005 and by 50 per cent by 2008. The most immediate goals are to reduce by 20 per cent the number of 11–16 year olds who use Class A drugs – basically LSD, ecstasy, heroin, cocaine and crack cocaine – and to delay the period of first use of such drugs by six months, all by 2002.

With school based surveys planned for each country in train and a new large-scale biannual national school survey across England, this monitoring is a sensible and appropriate way of beginning to measure drugs availability and rates of drug trying in under 16s. This programme should be excellent at measuring age of onset in consecutive age cohorts. However, although these surveys will be a valuable tool they will have serious limitations.

First, because they will utilize 'ever', past year and past month recency measures they will overestimate the number of regular 11–16 year old drug users. Yet, because of the way they will be administered they will probably dumb down full disclosure – particularly of heroin and crack cocaine. Moreover, by not following up non attenders they will have missing data for between 5 and 20 per cent of the secondary school age population. We have shown how non attenders, even without excludees, have higher rates of drug use than those in school on the day of administration. Although this will be a consistent deficit in the time series it will be an inaccurate measure of the real picture – of our cherished drugs realities. The groups with the most serious and regular drug use will be disproportionately absent in the audit. In particular attempts at measuring rates of heroin use through school and household surveys will be an exercise of dubious merit.

We have noted how age cohorts, as they pass through adolescence into young adulthood, have different rates of drug use and, indeed, slightly different chosen drugs repertoires. Moreover, even for the same age cohorts these repertoires change through time: for example, the switch away from ecstasy (Balding, 1999) towards cocaine. The planned national time series surveys cannot follow these age cohorts beyond 16. Yet, we know that 16–25 is the age range when most regular drug use kicks in and when the *use* of Class A drugs, particularly ecstasy and cocaine, grow. So if after the first survey we have 'worrying' rates of say cocaine use amongst the year 11, 16 year olds, how is this population to be followed up in 2003 to monitor whether target reductions have been achieved? Unfortunately there are no current solutions to this. The required monitoring tools such as longitudinal studies and a sophisticated national drugs household survey are simply unavailable.

This deficit in monitoring systems will be even more apparent in respect of the main 'problem' drug, heroin. Given concerns about the heroin outbreaks in Scotland and the English regions and the specific official targeting of this drug, we would want to have a benchmark on the prevalence of heroin use particularly in the 16–19 age group who are far less likely to be found in treatment data bases. There are no plans, primarily because of cost, to mount a plethora of regional mixed method studies like those we have described in Chapters 6 and 7 and, thereby, build up a national picture of heroin and heavy end poly drug use. The urine testing of arrestees, the regional drug misuse data bases and mortality rates will be of some help but again it is hard to see how baselines can be set and change monitored successfully – ironically for the most significant drug and group of problem drug users in the whole strategy.

The official answer to almost all queries about monitoring drug taking is that we have the British Crime Survey. As impressive and utilitarian as the drug misuse disclosures data in this household survey have been across the 1990s the new monitoring demands created by the national strategy cannot be met by it, even with tweaking. It is quite simply under powered, particularly in respect of 16–29 year olds. From measuring duration or frequency of drug use to identifying heroin and crack cocaine use, which is mostly found in deprived urban areas, this particular tool is found wanting. Most of its critics favour a national 'drug' household survey with far larger samples, booster samples and more sophisticated questioning (Gore, 1999; MacDonald, 1999).

Whatever the eventual 'solution' may be we must again face the fact that any informed debate about the efficacy of the drugs strategy even five years into its timetable (2002–03) will be hamstrung by equivocal and crude monitoring data. This will of course encourage endless political spin and perpetuate institutionalised dishonesty.

Stifling supply, distribution and availability of illegal drugs

This component of the drugs strategy is the least well publicly developed in each UK country probably because the key actors – the National Crime Squad, the National Criminal Intelligence Service and intelligence agencies shy away from public scrutiny leaving 'the police' and Customs and Excise as the more recognized players. It must also be said that evaluative tools are particularly poor, not in terms of sourcing and international supply knowledge but in how, for example, heroin is warehoused and distributed within the UK. The abolition of Regional Crime Squads and the introspection of local forces chasing their own performance targets rather than sharing in cross border policing (Porter, 1996) has meant that heroin and cocaine distribution mechanisms have been allowed to develop and bed in (Parker *et al.*, 1998a). Access to heroin has grown rapidly in Scotland and many English regions and in new geographical areas. Once established and with 'dependent' demand it always proves extremely hard to close down dealerships and prevent new ones springing up and avoid unintended public health consequences for example (Maher and Dixon, 1999).

Again belatedly official attention is now being given to mapping Class A drug distribution and mounting more corporate operations to stem flow around the UK. Although institutions such as prisons may well be able to protect themselves more effectively from drugs availability over the next few years, it seems highly unlikely that availability of all drugs can be reduced across the UK. While focusing on heroin and cocaine supply and distribution disruption may produce temporary or local gains (modest targets have been set), it is not expected, even within government, that significant progress will be made. Efforts to regear the economies where the poppy and cocoa plants grow have been in place for 20 years and, while a new concerted effort is underway, supply reduction cannot be expected for several years if at all (Stares, 1996). Increasing seizures of Class A drugs by 10 per cent, an immediate target, may be achieved but it would be surprising if this affected availability which is anyway remarkably hard to measure systematically. We would want to see reductions in offer/availability/access questions in school surveys, price increases and regular talk of 'droughts' via local inter-agency 'intelligence' before even beginning to believe that within a global economy and in a country with exceptionally high drug demand rates we can expect the supply of drugs to be stifled.

Delivering treatment gains with problem drug users

One of the most radical and most welcome shifts in priority found in the national plan involves a major commitment to improving and increasing treatment services to the point of expecting the Police service to become partners in treatment delivery. Unlike with the faith in primary prevention there is robust international research evidence that treatment works and that investment therein harvests real gains in health and crime reduction (Edmonds *et al.*, 1999; NTORS, 1999). However, we also know that the relative gains from treatment are dependent on the style, quality and specific regimes delivered by local treatment services and that waiting lists, length of retention in treatment, support and mentoring of service users and so on, also affect results and gains (Hough, 1996). In particular we know little about treatment outcomes for young people and cannot be certain that young person's services can deliver sustained gains.

In the UK there are further problems with delivering robust, high quality treatment services. First, the treatment sector is an 'unpopular' place to work. It does not routinely attract high calibre staff, parti-cularly doctors and competent team managers, who find the working conditions and lack of 'status' a deterrent. There is no recognized training route into drug services either through NVQ modular training levels or by further or higher education national awards as in nursing, teaching or social work. Moreover, because there has been little or no interest in modernising this sector across the 1990s, the current services are not quality assured or sufficiently audited and with notable exceptions a culture of mediocrity appears to have set in.

The other key problem or deficit in terms of upgrading this sector is that the lines of commissioning, defining and auditing street level services are confusing and indirect. There is local authority community care money alongside Lottery Board, Single Regeneration and European Social Fund money being used to fund, or more often prop up, services which are financed from central government via National Health Trusts. This all makes the transformation of services highly problematic even when new resources are made available. In short, the national plan relies on increasing treatment services by about a third in the first few years of the strategy (1998–2004) and on those services delivering what works. Yet the government has inherited inadequate delivery mechanisms and a treatment sector in desperate need of modernisation, new investment and a quality agenda.

A further uncertainty must be whether the emphasis on coercive treatment and reliance on the criminal justice system (Edmonds *et al.*, 1999) to deliver will undermine treatment gains. With the whole thrust of the strategy and nearly all the new investment targeted at the criminal justice process and the prisons, the strategy is stepping into the unknown. There is no doubting that substantial gains will be made from Arrest Referral and Treatment and Testing initiatives (Turnbull, 1999), but whether we can expect to achieve targets of 100 per cent gains in participation in treatment interventions which also must have a positive impact on health and crime by 2008 is doubtful. The fear must be that drug using offenders, not unlike the heroin users and alienated crack cocaine users we have described, may be suspicious, even cynical, about such initiatives particularly if their delivery is bedevilled by confused roles between the key professional groups (Newburn and Elliot, 1999) and often mediocre treatment regimes. Even if these treatment gains are achieved by some creative accounting with base lines, the public question will be has an extra £100 million (1999–2004) produced adequate returns and is the political commitment to on-going revenue flow still intact?

More generally under the treatment banner, there are several well conceived secondary goals. These include reducing Hepatitis B, reducing injecting and needle sharing among those already in treatment and requiring DATs to focus on waiting list times for community services and developing young persons' services. With further rhetoric about involving GPs in treatment and increasing detoxification facilities and at least identifying the need for vocational standards and quality markers among drugs workers, the recognition that the times ahead will be hard is clearly there. Although reducing drug related deaths is a separate aspirational goal, it will be well into the decade before any initiatives flow. We have argued earlier that failure to address this issue with practical interventions is a genuine case of official neglect.

In short there are too many 'unknowns' in this element of the national programme to make outcomes predictable. Theoretically this strand of the strategy has great potential. What seems likely is that the longer this initiative is allowed to run the more significant will be the gains particularly if all the attendant difficulties in driving the agenda through the multi-agency bureaucratic maze (Rumgay and Cowan, 1998) are constantly attended to.

New evaluative tools are being developed to assess this treatment delivery initiative ranging from urine testing arrestees on a rolling programme of site visits, NEW-ADAM (Bennett, 1998), monitoring arrest referral schemes (Edmonds *et al.*, 1999) and eventually assessing the Testing and Treatment Orders (Turnbull, 1999).

The increases in access to treatment in the wider community will be more difficult to both achieve and monitor, as will the gathering of robust evidence that treatment agencies are delivering on gains in health and crime reduction. There is no reliable measure of the numbers in treatment, given the frailties of the Department of Health's Misuse of Drugs Data Base which even after renovation will suffer from major non-compliance, particularly from GPs in respect of reporting treatment episodes.

Indeed even if the data base were comprehensive in capturing service users, due to long waiting lists, the *demand* for treatment is hard to gauge because potential entrants are put off by the delay or often do not attend (the DNAs) when their appointment eventually arrives. This also means that, in the short run at least, increases in treatment episodes monitored via the data base are poor indicators of real demand because capacity has not increased sufficiently to allow major surges in presentation to occur.

Reducing drug related anti-social and criminal behaviour

In many ways this element of strategy will be dependent upon the ability of the treatment sector to successfully expand and deliver its services and interventions to those netted in the criminal justice system. The detail within this thrust of the national plan is concerned with identifying problem drug users whose offending is directly related to their drugs 'problem'. There is absolutely no doubt that dependent drug use found in the UK's poor communities does generate additional crime (Hough, 1996). We have detailed this in Chapters 6 and 7 in respect of heroin, crack cocaine and poly drug use. We have also suggested that a new 'wave' of problem drug users is currently being generated in Scotland and some English regions via heroin and poly drug use which will make for additional challenges during the first half of this new decade.

There can be little argument with the logic of the strategy to try and identify these users through arrest referral schemes in police custody suites, Youth Offender Teams and through presentence assessments leading to the making of community based Treatment and Testing Orders and delivering help within the prison system (Brook *et al.*, 1998). Nor can there be any doubt about the commitment of the government's

Home Office led plans since they are supported by an additional £60 million for community interventions and £60 million for a prison programme – to be spent in the first few years of the decade. This is a significant investment and indeed for some an 'overkill' at the price of developing mainstream community drugs services which can also contribute to crime reduction (Parker and Kirby, 1996; NTORS, 1999). The targets which are set in the UK strategy are both explicit and highly ambitious. They include 25 per cent reduction in the levels of repeat offending by drug misusers by 2005 rising to 50 per cent by 2008 and reducing the number of arrestees urine testing positive for Class A drugs, notably heroin and cocaine (crack cocaine cannot easily be isolated) from 18 per cent to 15 per cent. There should be few difficulties in evaluating the effectiveness of these new programmes because monitoring systems will be set in place from the outset. The frustration is likely to be with slow, patchy implementation and then with attrition as individuals are lost from local Treatment and Testing projects either by disappearing or by incarceration. Moreover, it will be difficult to know whether upon completion of these mandatory programmes any gains in the reduction of Class A drug use and drug related crime are sustained. Prison leavers will prove the most difficult to monitor (Swan and James, 1998).

In respect of drug driving the strategy remains hamstrung by the difficulties in developing effective roadside tests for drug related impaired driving. We have no hesitation, based on our large-scale nightclub study (Chapter 5), in arguing that drug driving is far more prevalent than is publicly recognized (see also Automobile Association, 1998) and that very many more accidents and related threat to pedestrians and other drivers are drug related than official figures suggest.

Nightclubs are clearly seen in both central and local government worlds as a major cause of drug related anti-social and criminal behaviour. There has been new legislation to give local police and licensing committees powers to close down nightclubs with a 'transparent' drugs problem. We argued in Chapter 5 that this approach to some extent confuses the relationship between the effect of drugs, for example ecstasy, on customer behaviour and the more worrying role of local organized crime in the nightclub scene. Persecuting clubbers and certainly a proportion of responsible club owners–managers is a poor substitute for facing up to the really difficult problem of prosecuting local criminals whose preoccupations are with making money from drugs distribution, running door staff crews, 'taxing' club owners and even taking over certain clubs. There is also the likelihood that such a clampdown strategy will displace Class A drug use into the ever growing clusters of late night licence café bars found in most British cities. With further deregulation in opening hours this may well extend the acceptability of drinking *and* drug use being as 'time out' activity among the post adolescent–young adult customer base.

The Missing Elements

On the basis of our own analysis of UK drugs we have identified a number of areas where we conclude that strategic thinking is largely absent and policy and practice initiatives in short supply. We begin with these as they can be bolted onto the current strategy we have just outlined. Our other concerns – about the current legislation and institutionalised dishonesty – will, by definition, be rejected by the forces of conservatism.

Secondary prevention and public health

Aside from some initiatives in Scotland a crucial omission in the national plan is the absence of early interventions and explicit harm reduction initiatives. This is a consequence of the war on drugs approach of the 1990s, whereby, harm reduction was seen as a capitulation, an admission of failure: if you tell them how to take drugs more safely you are condoning their use. As we discussed in Chapter 6 this means that significant numbers of young, increasingly problematic drug users are staying 'hidden' and taking highly damaging drugs pathways to injecting poly drug use. Overdosing, dying from mishaps, becoming seriously unhealthy are all tied up in these emergent problem drug careers. The official indifference to all this is chilling and is the worst example of London centricity, whereby, if the rate of increases in drug related death rates being experienced in the north of Britain, for instance is more than the rate of fatal traffic accidents in Northumbria (Northumbria Police, 1999) were occurring south of Watford, responses would be quite different and far more urgent than is currently the case. Increases in drug related deaths, although being reviewed, only will be fully faced politically and strategically some four years into the national programme when practical measures to deal with methadone mishap, poly drug accidents and heroin related deaths should finally be introduced.

There is no doubt that secondary prevention initiatives are sanctioned in the strategy's small print, but it is quite clear that little thought has gone into how to develop and utilize such interventions and certainly there is no encouragement or enthusiasm in sight, despite authoritative recommendations of their necessity (Gossop *et al.*, 1998). Neither the night clubbers nor young problem users are likely to be targets of sustained secondary prevention programmes. The irony noted in Chapter 4 is that primary prevention initiatives actually have more secondary gains with current drug users than in preventing initiation.

'Respectable' over 25s and normalisation

The whole strategy in respect of preventing and reducing drug use focuses on under 25s. This is in line with the traditional notion that 'middle-class' twentysomethings begin to settle down and reduce their excesses, as car and home ownership, regular job with responsibilities and family making kick in, and, that working-class, drug using men with female partners also show signs of maturing out of deviant lifestyles (Graham and Bowling, 1995).

However, with an extended post adolescence and a longer journey to these structures of mature citizenship – notably delays in marriage and parenthood, more young adults living alone and in communal living arrangements with extended education and training and more career uncertainty – we can no longer assume greater conformity will impact as early. We have discussed, thus far, the largely indicative evidence that 1990s youth will take the normalisation of 'sensible' recreational drug use with them into this new decade and that the scale of drug involvement among twentysomethings may be greater than for previous age cohorts. Cannabis and stimulant drugs such as amphetamines and cocaine seem the likely drugs of choice until the next designer drug arrives. It is not just the traditional arenas of the nightclub and going out scenes (Chapter 5) and in the social exclusion zones (ACMD, 1998) where we will find such drug involvement but also in the social life of professional groups in particular (Ramsay and Partridge, 1999). This possible growth in occasional recreational drug use in conventional adult populations may pose some knotty dilemmas for government, not only in respect of 'defiance' through Class A and B drug use *per se* but also drug use and work, drug use and driving and drug use and parenting in particular. The national plan has, by focusing on cocaine (alongside heroin), set itself up for a debate it has barely prepared for beyond a footnote about workplace drug testing. This is largely because the thrust of the strategy focuses on the serious drug use which, in dis-advantaged communities, leads to crime and community insecurity that invite criminal justice–treatment interventions. The 'rising' work hard–play hard young professionals rather challenge all this. They also leave the strategy open to criticism: that it is not concerned so much with Class A drug use as with controlling people who live in the social exclusion zones and are involved in crime. That university students and successful high flyers do coke is a knotty problem for a strategy which equates drug use with being both a loser and engine of crime and disorder.

Our overall point is that here once again is a drugs reality, at the millennium which, because of institutional dishonesty, is not publicly accepted by government and which will expose the strategy in due course. There is no sense of the dynamism in the ever changing drugs landscape of the UK we have described being recognized in the national plan. While heroin use does largely remain a drug which is related to social exclusion, cocaine has a far broader appeal. Exposing its widespread use beyond the social exclusion zones, given the inevitable emphasis on measuring and monitoring who uses it, will make it more difficult for government to justify its current strategy and stance on legislation in respect of possessing and supplying illicit drugs. In a rational world some policy revision would be required to deal with these drugs realities.

Institutionalised Dishonesty

Disrespect for the Misuse of Drugs Act is remarkably widespread. This statute has probably been technically breached by the majority of 15–30 year olds in Scotland and England. With the Independent Inquiry into the Misuse of Drugs Act (Independent Inquiry, 2000) reporting the need for revision, after an impressive and extensive review of drugs enforcement legislation, we are reminded that statutes drafted at the end of the 1960s are still expected to be operationally effective thirty years later – but they are not. New Labour not only refuses to discuss how the drugs laws could be renovated, it thus far refuses to discuss the possibility of sanctioning any official review. It is difficult to think of any other area of government where senior ministers go to such lengths to ambush not only the modernisation of a statute but even a scrutiny of arrangements in a failing area of government.

Yet, we have seen how 'confused' young people are about the relative dangerousness of different substances, how the majority of young Britons break the current law, how policing and sanctions are a lottery and how definitions of supply are at stark odds with what young people define as 'sorting'. It is hard to conclude that none of this invites review, of the current legislation. It is equally hard to conclude that such a review, despite authoritative calls, will occur in the foreseeable future.

Although such a legislative review is an omission which needs high-lighting, this is but one more example of the institutionalised dishonesty about discussing and managing drug use and misuse we have had to keep referring to. We have documented too many examples of 'eco-nomies with the truth' for comfort, simply by comparing drugs realities with official discourse. Dissonance is found in definitions and interpreta-tions of: how young people obtain their drugs; how young people make drugs decisions; the efficacy of drugs education; the utility of early harm reduction; the social and health effects of recreational drug use; the nature of drugs–crime relationships, and so on. While there are signs that greater honesty and realism are beginning to percolate into official dis-course, the effects of institutionalised dishonesty will take many years to repair and the dangers of official relapse remain, particularly, when the politics of re-election come around every few years.

Monitoring and Managing UK Drugs More Effectively

Setting up monitoring systems

Drugs policy is in its infancy as an arm of governance. Its development across the last century was largely reactive, built up on the basis of responding to drugs 'problems' as they emerged. The pace of this has clearly quickened in the last 25 years but reactiveness has continued to be the modus operandi. Even prevention programmes which may be seen as proactive are in fact gaining significance as a politically acceptable response to the rising rates of drug trying and drug use among young Britons.

One way of attempting to end this catch up approach to state inter-vention is to put far more effort into applied research and monitoring and begin to model how the drugs landscape changes through time and attempt to develop early warnings and forecasts for the future. In fact compared with most of Europe the UK already has a large portfolio of drugs related research (Fountain and Griffiths, 1997). There has been a strong research focus in Scotland and England but less so in Wales. In Northern Ireland such research is only just beginning. However, this is not the same as purposeful, systematic investment in research and monitoring to build up a moving picture of Drugs UK.

In each UK country money has been set aside for both monitoring and evaluating the national plan and making better assessments of the drugs landscape. Unfortunately, given the inadequacies of present research and monitoring systems and previous under investment the genuine improvements which will occur will still be inadequate. We have eluded to the evaluation problems for the strategies earlier. Here we look at plans for the future.

In Scotland, Wales and England there was, until November 1999, due to be an extension in the voluntary urine testing of arrestees in policy custody suites. The piloting phase of this programme in England (Bennett, 1998) showed rates of opiate and increasingly cocaine/crack cocaine residues in 20–50 per cent of arrestees in different regions. In the Scottish piloting cocaine/crack cocaine had not joined the opiates in the country's arrestees.

As originally conceived this programme, NEW-ADAM in England and Wales, was to provide important monitoring information about drugs–crime connections, changing drug taking repertoires and regional differences in drugs consumption. Then, in November 1999, New Labour engaged in an unplanned political manoeuvre which may undermine this initiative and consequently extensive developmental and commissioning plans – making urine testing of arrestees mandatory. In practice this will mean giving the police discretion to urine test whoever they 'suspect' of drug use, some would say, whoever they want. This is a further example of the political processes we have discussed which have, are and increasingly will undermine the integrity of the national plan. This draconian move will, in the long run, if extensively utilized, probably extend the national monitoring potential of urine testing but will have numerous unintended consequences for the whole drugs interventions strategy in the criminal justice system. As ever these will emerge slowly and political culpability will be lost.

In England an annual survey of the perceptions of Drug Action Teams will provide useful regional and local pictures of the drugs situation. If well administered and analysed this will be a vital addition to developing 'early warnings' and mapping the epidemiology of changing drugs trends. There are also plans to commission a handful of community studies of hidden or difficult to reach drug using populations, much like the crack cocaine study described in the last chapter. It is unlikely these will be of sufficient number and sophistication to fully describe the more hidden worlds we eluded to in the previous few chapters but they will nevertheless be of value. What will remain in short supply, because of their cost, are detailed studies of cities and towns struggling with a serious problem drug population. Capture–recapture studies which describe and estimate the number of problem drug users in a particular community have always found more problem users than official indicators show, but they are expensive to undertake and will not be regarded as good value at the centre despite being invaluable locally (Hay and McKeganey, 1999; Parker *et al.*, 1988).

Other likely monitoring and 'early warning' initiatives will include copying *Pulsecheck* in the USA whereby drugs 'experts' and commentators pool their knowledge and perceptions of how the drugs landscape may be changing. The prospects of this initiative being sufficiently developed and co-ordinated to produce the vital UK perspective are unclear however, given the national priorities and preferences within the kingdom. The irony is that drugs distribution shows no respect for national jurisdictions and that, for instance, not seeing Scotland and Northern England as being part of the same developing heroin problem remains an epidemiological mistake. Finally it is possible that a British DAWN system of monitoring drug related incidents seen in accident and emergency units will eventually be set up.

All in all there are clearly going to be significant improvements in monitoring and data collection over the next few years. Probably from around 2002–03 the potential to begin public forecasting will be there. Thereafter if this approach is sustained and used purposefully and imaginatively there is a real possibility that UK drugs can be more successfully mapped and its dynamism described and harnessed for more effective management and policy development.

Forecasting with science and intuition

We have shown how watching and commentating on UK drugs cannot be a wholly scientific exercise. Drug use because it is illegal is a largely hidden activity. This ensures data gathering is problematic and traditional scientific rules about sampling, 'control groups' and the like must often be waived. If we are to model and forecast and so try to predict how the drugs landscape is shifting, then we must also be intuitive, not by applying common sense but by seeking out trends and patterns and repetitions from drugs history and slowly evolving epidemiological models. For instance North American commentators have shown us how the heroin cycle operates (Hunt and Chambers, 1976) and how cocaine and crack cocaine consumption is linked (Johnson, 1999) and how there may well be cyclical–epidemiological relationship between heroin and cocaine consumption (Inciardi and Harrison, 1998; Jacobs, 1999). To this we must add the particular cultural and social tendencies toward psycho-active consumption in a particular society, as we described in Chapter 1 but also recognize that interventions can occasionally influence future 'population' drugs decisions and behaviour.

Constructing a veracious forecasting system is clearly many years away. However what we can already do is identify likely scenarios. We can set up outline forecasts, crude hypotheses, which can prompt the evolving monitoring and forecasting system to focus on and test out a prediction of say a new drugs trend or an increasing type of morbidity.

We have made several such predictions based on the research studies described earlier. We re-explore three of those predictions by way of illustrating how a forecasting system might routinely work and how inadequate present arrangements are. First, we have suggested that 1990s British youth, as they move into their twenties, may take some of their drugs involvement with them and that rates of recent use may thus increase for this age group compared with previous twentysomething cohorts. We are not confident we know exactly what drugs this will involve beyond cannabis and cocaine or how significant all this will be. We simply note that there are good social scientific and policy reasons for carefully monitoring and assessing the drugs consumption behaviour of this age group during the decade and reviewing the current 'under 25s' only targeting.

Second, we have identified what we believe to be small but significant increases in heroin trying and use among youth populations in small cities and towns outside the 'old heroin' metropolitan areas. We have tried to understand through a brief national audit and qualitative interviewing what processes are involved. We have also tried to give early warning of the middle term consequences of new heroin outbreaks. If there was a research and monitoring programme in place whereby forecasting was a routine activity, our 'prompt' would have been followed up impartially and assessed by the key actors and expert use of appropriate data systems: local intelligence, seizures, treatment presentation, urine testing, morbidity and 'emergency' presentations, mortality and on-going community studies. In reality official responses in government have been contradictory and confused, veering from wholehearted endorsement (Parker *et al.*, 1998a) to outright denial (Ramsay and Partridge, 1999). The end result – do nothing.

Third, we have suggested that the increases in cocaine powder use in the younger adult population over recent years, may also generate increases in crack cocaine use among a minority. In time this minority are likely to become problem poly drug users or labelled as sufferers of co-morbidity. We have also pondered on whether heroin *and* crack cocaine may join together in heavy end careers and expressed concerns about what this may mean for problem drug use particularly in our larger cities. Again we know enough to know we cannot predict exactly how this will unfold. It is a worst scenario not to be sensationalised but again to act as a cue to drugs data gathering, monitoring and critical analysis within a forecasting framework. Currently we have almost no way of knowing what is unfolding without many more community research studies or better monitoring. School and household surveys are poor assessors of heroin and crack cocaine use and even urine testing programmes cannot distinguish crack from cocaine powder use. We know that crack users are less likely to present for treatment even if the regional databases were effective monitors. Again it is hardly surprising in the absence of accurate information that the drugs interventions industry has not been better prompted to provide more provision for problem stimulant users.

In summary, we are, at best, several years away from having adequate multi-method data to help us forecast how UK drugs are changing. What drugs research can already do is offer cues and prompts as to what arenas or trends or unexpected outcomes should be focused on, both in the absence of adequate drugs data and eventually when a more soph-isticated forecasting system is constructed.

UK drugs futures

UK drugs is now so established and trends so clearly set over many years that our final forecast is unequivocal. There is no prospect of radical reductions in overall drugs availability or rates of recreational or prob-lem drug use occurring over the next few years. This in turn means that there is little prospect of the drugs strategy genuinely delivering on the majority of its performance targets in the foreseeable future. The UK trends in drugs supply and demand – consumption has taken many years to bed in and is not susceptible to any interventions by the state demanding sudden and dramatic downturns. The politically astute time to set aspirational goals is when a robust interventions structure is in place and when particular types of drugs consumption, having risen, are plateauing or when certain age cohorts of younger people are show-ing signs of collective disinterest in respect of drugs consumption. Today's early adolescents may help out in a few years but contemporary late adolescents and twentysomethings are likely to be contrary. We have shown how adolescent drug trying has been rising, how post adoles-cents are embracing alcohol *and* illicit drugs to enhance time out and how more problematic drug use is developing in ever younger, susceptible minorities of youth. There are few signs in the drugs research community's knowledge book that these upward trends will change quickly or that official interventions can affect a significant downturn.

Yet, all this said the new UK drugs strategy is a break with the dark and dismal past. It is transparent, ambitious and, at least for now, relatively resource wealthy. It is able to distinguish between drugs and types of drug use and it entrusts its evolution to increasing reliance on evaluating what works. If it can overcome the operational inefficiencies of 'partnership' (Marlow and Pearson, 1999), be protected from the warriors and forces of conservatism, especially at re-election time, then it can become the foundation for an increasingly effective drugs strategy. Such a strategy will largely abandon the search for abstinence and 'solutions' in favour of management strategies. In a democratic, post industrial, globally influenced society the state can only mediate and minimise the excesses and harm of problematic drug use and warn against the downsides of recreational drug use. The development of a realistic strategy is underway but it will be several years before any consistency and integrity bed in. In the meantime government should be grateful that most drug use in the UK is recreational and relatively benign and that young Britons who do drugs manage to self regulate and stay safe *despite* not because of the state.

Bibliography

ACMD (1998) *Drug Misuse and the Environment*, Advisory Council on the Misuse of Drugs, Home Office, London.

Addiction Research (1994) Cocaine in the Community: International Perspectives Special Issue 2, 1.

Akram, G. and M. Galt (1999) 'A profile of harm-reduction practices and co use of illicit and licit drugs amongst users of dance drugs' *Drugs education, prevention and policy* 6, 2, pp. 215–26.

Aldridge, J., H. Parker and F. Measham (1999) *Drug Trying and Drug Use Across Adolescence*, Drugs Prevention Initiative Green Series Paper 24, Home Office, London.

Aldridge, J. and H. Parker (1998) *Patterns and profiles of young people and drug use. The feasibility of Identifying risk factors*, Drug Prevention Initiative, Home Office (unpublished).

Automobile Association (1998) *Drugs and Driving; a discussion paper*, Group Public Policy, Automobile Association, Basingstoke.

Balding, J. (1999) *Young People in 1998*, Exeter University, Exeter.

Barnard, M., A. Forsyth and N. McKeganey (1996) 'Levels of drug use among a sample of Scottish schoolchildren', *Drugs: education, prevention and policy* 3, 1, pp. 81–96.

Bean, P. and Y. Pearson (1992) 'Cocaine and Crack in Nottingham 1989–92' in J. Mott (ed.) *Crack Cocaine in England*, Home Office RPU Paper 70, London.

Bell, R., S. Pavis, S. Cunningham-Burley and A. Amos (1998) 'Young men's use of cannabis: exploring changes in meaning and context over time', *Drugs: education, prevention and policy* 5, 2, pp. 141–57.

Bennett, T. (1998) *Drug Testing Arrestees* Home Office Research Findings 70, London.

Bloor, M. and F. Wood (1998) (eds) *Issues in Problem Drug Use and Addictions*, Jessica Kingsley, London.

Boys, A., J. Fountain, P. Griffiths, J. Marsden, G. Stillwell and J. Strang (1998) *Making decisions: a qualitative study of young people, drugs and alcohol*, Health Education Authority, London.

Boys, A., J. Marsden and P. Griffith (1999) 'Reading between the Lines', *Druglink*, Jan/Feb, pp. 20–3.

Brain, K., H. Parker and T. Bottomley (1998) *Evolving Crack Cocaine Careers*, Home Office Publications Unit, London.

Branigan, P., H. Kuper and K. Wellings (1997) *The evaluation of the London dance safety campaign*, School of Hygiene and Tropical Medicine, London.

Branigan, P. and K. Wellings (1999) 'Acceptance of the harm reduction message in London Clubs and Underground system', *Drugs education, prevention and policy* 6, 3, pp. 389–99.

Brooke, D., C. Taylor, J. Gunn and A. Maden (1998) 'Substance misusers remanded to prison – a treatment opportunity', *Addiction* V93, 12, pp. 1851–7.

Brown, J. and I. Kreft (1998) 'Zero effects of drug prevention programmes', *Evaluation Review*, 22, pp. 3–4.

Brunswick, A. and S. Titus (1999) 'Heroin Patterns and Trajectories in an African American cohort (1969–1990)' in J. Inciardi and L. Harrison *Heroin in the Age of Crack Cocaine*, Thoms and Oakes, Sage.

Cabinet Office (1999) *First Annual Report and National Plan* United Kingdom Anti Drugs Coordination Unit, London.

Cabinet Office (1998) *Tackling Drugs to Build a Better Britain*, Cabinet Office, London.

Calafat, A. (1998) *Nightlife in Europe and recreative drug use in Palma de Majorca*, SONAR 98 IREFREA/European Commission, Palma de Majorca.

Caulkins, J., C. Rydell, F. Everingham, J. Chiesa and S. Bushway (1999) *An Ounce of Prevention, a Pound of Uncertainty: The Cost Effectiveness of School Based Drug Prevention Programmes*, RAND, Santa Monica, California.

Coffield, F. and L. Gofton (1994) *Drugs and Young People*, Institute for Public Policy Research, London.

Committee of Public Accounts (1999) *Fifteenth Report: HM Customs and Excise: the prevention of Drug Smuggling*, House of Commons (35), London.

Coombs, R. and D. Ziedonis (eds) (1995) *Handbook on Drug Abuse Prevention*, Allyn and Bacon.

De Alceron, R. (1969) 'The spread of heroin in a community', *Bulletin in Narcotics*, July–Sept. pp. 17–22.

Ditton, J. and R. Hammersley (1996) *A Very Greedy Drug: Cocaine in Context*, Harwood, London.

Donmall, M., N. Seivewright, J. Douglas, T. Draycott and T. Millar (1996) *National Cocaine Treatment Study*, Report to the Department of Health's Task Force to Review Services for Drug Misusers, London.

Dorn, N. and K. Murji (1992) *Drug Prevention: a review of the English language literature*, Research Monograph 5, Institute for the Study of Drug Dependence, London.

Dorn, N., J. Ribbens and N. South (1987) *Coping with a nightmare: family feelings about long term drug use*, ISDD, London.

Drugs (1998) 'Drug use among vulnerable groups of young people', *Drugs Education Prevention and Policy* V5, 3 (Special Issue).

Edmonds, M., M. Hough, P. Turnbull and T. May (1999) *Doing Justice to Treatment*, DPAS Paper 2, Home Office, London.

Edmonds, M., M. Hough and N. Urquia (1996) *Tackling Drug Markets*, Police Research Group, Paper 80, Home Office, London.

Egginton, R. and H. Parker (2000) *Hidden Heroin Users: Young People's Unchallenged Journeys to Problematic Drug Use*, Drug Scope, London.

Elland-Goossenson, A., T. Hak and L. Vollemans (1998) 'Heroin Addiction Careers: downward spiral or controlled descent?' *Contemporary Drug Problems*, Summer, pp. 293–319.

EMCDDA (1999) *Drugs Problems in the European Union: Annual Report*, European Monitoring Centre for Drugs and Drug Addiction, Lisbon.

ESPAD (1997) *Alcohol and Other Drug Use Among Students in 26 European Countries*, Swedish Council on Alcohol and Other Drugs, Stockholm.

Fazey, C. (1987) *The Evaluation of the Liverpool Drug Dependency Clinic*, 1985–87 Mersey Regional Health, Liverpool.

Finch, J. (1999) 'Death dance of the disco' *Guardian*, 23 January.

Finnigan, F. (1996) 'How non heroin users perceive heroin users and how heroin users perceive themselves', *Addiction Research* 4, 1, pp. 25–32.

Forsyth, A. (1996) 'Places and patterns of drug use in the Scottish dance scene', *Addiction* 91, 4, pp. 511–21.

Forsyth, A. (1998) *A Quantitative Study of DanceDrug Use*, Ph.D. Glasgow University.

Fountain, J. and P. Griffiths (1997) *Inventory, bibliography and synthesis of qualitative research (drugs) in the EU*, EMCDDA, Lisbon.

Gay, M. *et al.* (1985) *The Interim Report*, Avon Drugs Abuse Monitoring Project, Hartcliffe Health Centre, Bristol.

Goddard, E. and V. Higgins (1999) *Smoking, drinking and drug use among young teenagers in 1998*, Office of National Statistics, London.

Gore, S. (1999) 'Effective Monitoring of Young People's Use of Illegal Drugs', *British Journal of Criminology* 39, 4, pp. 575–603.

Gossop, M., P. Griffiths, B. Powis and J. Strang (1994) 'Cocaine: Patterns of use routes of administration and severity of dependence', *British Journal of Psychiatry* 164, pp. 660–4.

Gossop, M., J. Marsden, D. Stewart, P. Lehmann, C. Edward, A. Wilson and G. Segar (1998) 'Substance use, health and social problems of service users at 54 drug treatment agencies', *British Journal of Psychiatry* 173, pp. 166–71.

Graham, J. and B. Bowling (1995) *Young People and Crime*, Home Office Research Study 145, Home Office, London.

Griffiths, P., M. Gossop, B. Powis and J. Strang (1994) 'Transitions in patterns of heroin administration', *Addiction* 89, pp. 301–9.

Griffiths, P., M. Gossop, B. Powis and J. Strang (1993) 'Reaching hidden populations of drug users by privilaged access interviewers', *Addiction* 88, pp. 1617–26.

Griffiths, P., L. Vingoe, K. Jansen, J. Sherval, R. Lewis and R. Hartnoll (1997) *New Trends in Synthetic Drugs in the European Union*, EMCDDA, Lisbon.

Hammersley, R., J. Ditton, I. Smith and E. Short (1999) 'Patterns of Ecstasy Use by Drug Users', *British Journal of Criminology* 39, 4, pp. 625–47.

Hammersley, R. and V. Morrison (1987) 'Effects of poly drug use on criminal activities of heroin users', *British Journal of Addiction* Vol. 82.

Handy, C., R. Pater and A. Barrowcliff (1998) 'Drug use in South Wales: who uses Ecstasy anyway?', *Journal of Substance Misuse* 3, pp. 82–8.

Hart, L. and N. Hunt (1997) *Choosers not Losers?*, Invecta Community Care NHS, Kent.

Hartnoll, R., R. Lewis and M. Mitchenson (1985) *Drug Problems Assessing Local Needs*, Drug Indicators Project, London.

HAS (1996) *Children and Young People: substance misuse services*, Health Advisory Service, London.

Haw, S. (1985) *Drug Problems in Greater Manchester*, Glasgow, SCODA.

Hay, G. and N. McKeganey (1999) *Capture-recapture estimates of drug misuse in urban and non urban settings in the north east of Scotland*, Centre for Drug Misuse Research, University of Glasgow.

HEA (1999) *Drug Use in England*, Health Education Authority, London.

Health Promotion Agency for Northern Ireland (1996) *Illicit drug use in Northern Ireland: A Handbook for Professionals*, Belfast.

Hirst, J. and A. McCameley-Finney (1994) *The Place and Meaning of Drugs in the Lives of Young People*, Sheffield Hallam University, Sheffield.

HMSO (1994) *Tackling Drugs Together*, Her Majesty's Stationery Office, London.

Home Office (1999).

Hough (1996) *Problem Drug Use and Criminal Justice*, London: Drugs Prevention Initiative.

Hughes, P. (1977) *Behind the Wall of Respect*, University of Chicago Press, Chicago.

Hunt, L. and C. Chambers (1976) *The Heroin Epidemics: A study of Heroin Use in the United States*, Spectrum, New York.

Hunter, G., M. Donogheu and G. Stimson (1995) 'Crack use and injection on the increase among injecting drug users in London', *Addiction* 99, 1397–400.

Inciardi, J. and L. Harrison (1998) *Heroin in the Age of Crack Cocaine*, Sage Thousand Oaks.

Inciardi, J. (1994) 'Recent research on crack cocaine/crime correction', *Crime and Crime Prevention* 3, pp. 63–82.

Independent Inquiry (2000) *Drugs and the Law*, Report of the Independent Inquiry into the Misuse of Drugs Act 1971.

ISDD (1994) *Paying for Heroin*, Institute for the Study of Drug Dependence, London.

Jacobs, B. (1999) 'Crack to Heroin? Drug markets and transition', *British Journal of Criminology* 39, 4, pp. 555–73.

Johnson, B. (1999) *Crack Distribution and Abuse in New York*, Paper to Anglo-American Workshop on Drug Markets, John Jay College, New York.

Johnson, B., M. Natarajan, E. Dunlap and E. Elmoghzy (1994) 'Crack Abusers and Non Crack Abusers: Profiles of Drug Use, Drug Sales and Non Drug Criminality', *The Journal of Drug Issues* 24, 1, pp. 117–41.

Johnston, C., M. Pentz, M. Weber, J. Dwyer, N. Baer, D. Mackinnon and W. Hansen (1990) 'Relative Effectiveness of Comprehensive Community Programming for Drug Abuse Prevention with High Risk and Low Risk Adolescents', *Journal of Consulting and Clinical Psychology* V58, 4, pp. 447–56.

Kaye, S., S. Darke and R. Finlay-Jones (1998) 'The onset of heroin use and criminal behaviours: does order make a difference?', *Drug and Alcohol Dependence* 53, pp. 79–84.

Kearney, P. and M. Ibbetson (1991) 'Opiate dependent women and their babies', *British Journal of Social Work* 21, pp. 105–26.

Kleber, H. (1988) 'Epidemic Cocaine Abuse: America's Present, Britain's Future', *British Journal of Addiction* 85, pp. 1351–71.

Klee, H. and J. Morris (1994) 'Factors that lead young amphetamine misusers to seek help', *Drugs: education, prevention and policy* 1, 3, pp. 289–97.

Klenka, H. (1986) 'Babies born in a district general hospital to mothers taking heroin', *British Medical Journal* Vol.293, pp. 745–6.

Kohn, M. (1997) 'The Chemical Generation and its Ancestors: dance crazes and drug panics across eight decades', *The International Journal of Drug Policy* 8, 3, pp. 137–42.

MacDonald, Z. (1999) 'Illicit Drug Use in the UK', *British Journal of Criminology* 39, 4, pp. 585–603.

Maher, L. and D. Dixon (1999) 'Policing and Public Health', *British Journal of Criminology* 39, 4, pp. 488–512.

Makhoul, M., F. Yates and S. Wolfson (1998) 'A survey of substance use at a UK university: prevelance of use and views of students', *Journal of Substance Misuse* 3, pp. 119–24.

Marlow, A. and G. Pearson (1999) *Young people, drugs and community safety*, Russell House, Lyme Regis.

McCauley, A. (1994) *The Emergence of Crack Cocaine in Inner City Sheffield*, CRESCR, Sheffield Hallam University.

McElrath, K. and K. McEvoy (1999) *Ecstasy use in Northern Ireland*, Queens University, Belfast.

McKeganey, N. and M. Barnard (1992) *Aids, Drugs and Sexual Risk*, Open University Press, Buckingham.

McKeganey, N. (1999) '*Pre-teen Drug Users in Scotland*', *Addiction Research*, Vol.7, 6, pp. 493–507.

Measham, F., J. Aldridge and H. Parker (2000) *Dancing on Drugs: Risk health and hedonism in the British club scene*, Free Association Books, London.

Measham, F., H. Parker and J. Aldridge (1998) *Starting, Switching, Slowing, Stopping*, Home Office, Drugs Prevention Initiative, Green Series Paper 21, London.

Meikle, A., C. McCallum, A. Marshall and G. Coster (1996) *Drugs Survey on a Selection of Secondary School Pupils in the Glasgow Area Aged 13–16*, Glasgow Drugs Prevention Team, Glasgow.

Merchant, J. and R. Macdonald (1994) 'Youth and the Rave Culture, Ecstasy and Health', *Youth and Policy* 45, pp. 16–38.

Miller, P. and M. Plant (1996) 'Drinking, Smoking and Illicit Drug Use Among 15 and 16 year olds in the United Kingdom', *British Medical Journal* 313, pp. 394–7.

Morris, S. (1998) *Clubs, Drugs and Doormen*, Police Research Group, Paper 86, Home Office, London.

Newburn, T. and J. Elliot (1999) *Risks and Responses: drug prevention and youth justice*, DPAS, Home Office, London.

Northern Ireland Drugs Campaign (1999) *Drug Strategy for Northern Ireland*, Belfast.

Northumbria Police (1999) *Raids Target Heroin Supply*, Newcastle upon Tyne.

NTORS (1999) *NTORS: Two Year Outcomes. Changes in Substance Use, Health and Crime*, Department of Health, London.

O'Connor, J. and B. Saunders (1992) 'Drug Education: An Appraisal of a Popular Preventive', *The International Journal of the Addiction* V27, pp. 165–85.

Parker, H., J. Aldridge and F. Measham (1998) *Illegal Leisure: the normalisation of adolescent recreational drug use*, Routledge, London. (Reprinted 1999.)

Parker, H., C. Bury and R. Egginton (1998a) *New Heroin Outbreaks Amongst Young People in England and Wales*, Police Research Group, Home Office, London.

Parker, H. and T. Bottomley (1996) *Crack Cocaine and Drugs – Crime Careers*', Home Office Publications Unit, London.

Parker, H. and P. Kirby (1996) *Methadone Maintenance and Crime Reduction on Merseyside*, Police Research Group, Crime Prevention Series, Home Office, London.

Parker, H., K. Bakx and R. Newcombe (1988) *Living with Heroin: the impact of a heroin epidemic on an English community*, Open University Press, Buckingham.

Parker, H. and R. Newcombe (1987) 'Heroin use and acquisitive crime in an English community', *British Journal of Sociology* Vol.38, 3, pp. 331–50.

Pearson, G. (1987) *The New Heroin Users*, Basil Blackwell, Oxford.

Pearson, G. and K. Patel (1988) 'Drugs, Deprivation and Ethnicity: Outreach among Asian drug users in a northern English city', *Journal of Drug Issues*, 28, 1, pp. 199–224.

Pentz, M. (1993) 'Comparative Effects of Community-Based Drug Abuse Protection' in Beer, J., G. Marlatt and R. McMahon (eds) *Addictive Behaviours Across the Life Span: Prevention, Treatment and Policy Issues*, Sage, London.

Perri 6, B. Jupp, H. Perry and K. Laskey (1997) *The Substance of Youth*, Joseph Rowntree Foundation, York.

Petridis, A. (1996) 'How much Ecstasy do the British really take?', *Mixmag* 2, 62, July, pp. 98–100.

Pirie, M. and R. Worcester (1999) *The Next Leaders?*, Adam Smith Institute, London.

Plant, E. and M. Plant (1999) 'Primary prevention for young children: a comment on the UK government's 10 year drug strategy', *International Journal of Drug Policy* 10, pp. 385–401.

Porter, M. (1996) *Tackling cross border crime*, Police Research Group, Home Office, London.

Power, R. and R. Hartnou (1992) 'The role of significant life events in discriminating help seeking among illicit drug users', *The International Journal of the Addictions* 17, 9, pp. 1019–34.

POST (1996) *Common Illegal Drugs and their Effects: cannabis, ecstasy, amphetamines and LSD*, Parliamentary Office of Science and Technology, London.

Ramsay, M. and S. Partridge (1999) *Drug Misuse Declared in 1998: results from the British Crime Survey*, Home Office Research Study 197, London.

Reid, M., J. Mickalian, K. Delucchi, S. Hall and P. Berger (1998) 'An acute dose of nicotine enhances cue-induced cocaine craving', *Drug and Alcohol Dependence* 49, pp. 95–104.

Release (1997) *Release drugs and dance survey*, Release, London.

Rumgay, J. and S. Cowan (1998) 'Pitfalls and Prospects in Partnership; Probation Programmes for Substance Misusing Offenders', *The Howard Journal* 37, 2, pp. 124–36.

Rutter, M. and D. Smith (1994) (eds) *Psycho-Social Disorder: Young People*, John Wiley, Chicester.

SCODA (1999) *Managing and making policy for drug related incidents in schools*, SCODA, London.

The Scottish Office (1998) *Tackling Drugs in Scotland: Action in partnership*, Edinburgh.

Sherlock, K. (1998) 'Nightlife in Europe: Manchester' in A. Calafat (1998) *Nightlife in Europe and recreative drug use in Palma de Majorca*, SONAR 98, REFREA/European Commission, Palma de Majorca.

Shewan, D., P. Dalgarno and G. Reith (2000) 'Perceived risk and risk reduction among ecstasy users: the role of drug, set and setting', *International Journal of Drug Policy* 10 (2000) pp. 431–53.

Shiner, M. and T. Newburn (1997) 'Definitely, Maybe Not? The normalisation of recreational drug use amongst young people', *Sociology* V31, 3, pp. 511–29.

Shiner, M. and T. Newburn (1996) *Young People, Drugs and Peer Awareness*, Home Office DPI Paper 13, London.

Sloboda, Z. (1999) 'Problems for the Future? Drug use among vulnerable groups of young people', *Drugs education, prevention and policy* 6, 2, pp. 195–202.

SSI (1997) *Substance misuse and young people*, Social Services Inspectorate, London.

Stares, P. (1996) *Global Habit: the drug problem in a borderless world*, Brooklyn Institute, Washington.

Stimson, G., H. Pickering, A. Green, R. Foster and R. Power (1993) *Patterns and Trends in Cocaine and Crack Use in England and Wales*, 1990–92 Home Office, London.

Strang, J., B. Powis, D. Best, L. Vingoe, P. Griffiths, C. Taylor, S. Welch and M. Gossop (1999) 'Preventing opiate overdose fatalities with take-home naloxone: pre-launch study of possible impact and acceptability', *Addiction* 94, 2, pp. 199–204.

Stutman, R. (1989) 'Crack Stories from the States', *Druglink* 5, 4, pp. 6–7.

Sumner, C. (1994) *The Sociology of Deviance: An Obituary*, Open University Press, Buckingham.

Swan, R. and P. James (1998) 'The effect of the prison environment upon inmate drug taking behaviour', *The Howard Journal* 37, 3, pp. 252–65.

Turnbull, P. (1999) *Drug treatment and testing orders – interim evaluation*, Home Office, London.

Van de Wijngaart, G., R. Braan, D. de Bruin, M. Fris, N. Maalste and H. Verbraeck (1998) *Ecstasy in het uitgaanscircuit*, Addiction Research Institute, Utrecht University.

Walters, G. (1994) *Drugs and Crime in Lifestyle Perspective*, Sage, Thousand Oaks.

Webb, E., C. Ashton, D. Kelly and F. Kamali (1996) 'Alcohol and Drug use in UK university students', *Lancet* 348, pp. 922–5.

White, D and M. Pitts (1998) 'Educating young people about drugs: a systematic review', *Addiction* 93(10), pp. 1475–87.

Williamson, S., M. Gossop, B. Powis, P. Griffiths, J. Fountain and J. Strang (1997) 'Adverse effects of stimulant drugs in a community sample of drug users', *Drug and Alcohol Dependence* 44, pp. 87–94.

Winstock, A. (2000) 'Risky behavioural harm reduction amongst 1151 clubbers' Paper to *11th International Conference on the Reduction of Drug Related Harm*, Jersey.

Wright, S. and H. Klee (1999) 'A profile of amphetamine users who present to treatment services and do not return', *Drugs: education prevention and policy* 6, 2, pp. 227–42.

Young, L. and R. Jones (1997) *Young People and Drugs*, SHADO, Liverpool.

Index